Uta Gräf's Effortless Dressage Program

Also by Uta Gräf & Friederike Heidenhof

The Joy of Dressage 1: Motivating the Horse **(DVD)**

The Joy of Dressage 2: Training the Rider **(DVD)**

The Joy of Dressage 3: Competitive Success **(DVD)**

Uta Gräf and Friederike Heidenhof

Uta Gräf's Effortless Dressage Program

Lightness, Harmony, and Success Through Play, Groundwork, Trail Riding, and Turnout

Translated by Coralie Hughes

TRAFALGAR SQUARE
North Pomfret, Vermont

First published in the English language in 2016 by
Trafalgar Square Books
North Pomfret, Vermont 05053

Originally published in the German language as *Feines Reiten in der Praxis* by FNverlag der Deutschen Reiterlichen Verienigung GmbH, Warendorf

Disclaimer of Liability
The authors and publisher shall have neither liability nor responsibility to any person or entity with respect to any loss or damage caused or alleged to be caused directly or indirectly by the information contained in this book. While the book is as accurate as the authors can make it, there may be errors, omissions, and inaccuracies.

Trafalgar Square Books encourages the use of approved safety helmets in all equestrian sports and activities.

ISBN: 978 1 57076 772 2
Library of Congress Control Number: 2016950559

Photographs by Cavallo/Lisa Rädlein, Stuttgart (p. 2); EQUITANA/Sven Cramer, Düsseldorf (p. 101); Werner Ernst, Ganderkesee (p. 30); Eurodressage.com/Dr. Astrid Appels, Mol/Belgien (p. 80 *bottom*); Foto-Design gr. Feldhaus, Osnabrück (p. 140 *top*); Joachim Fleish, Weisenheim (p. 78); Friederike Heidenhof, Krefeld (pp. v *top and middle left*), ix, xi, xiii, xiv, xvi *top left and right, bottom right*, xvii, xviii *top and bottom left*, xix, xxi, xxii, 1, 4 *bottom*, 5 *bottom*, 7, 10, 11, 13, 19, 22, 23 *left*, 26, 27, 30, 31, 39, 41, 42, 43, 44, 48, 49, 50, 67, 68 *top left and right and bottom*, 69 *left*, 76 *top*, 82, 86, 88 *top and top middle*, 92, 96, 97, 98, 104 *left and right*, 107 *right*, 108 *bottom left*, 109 *top right and middle left and right*, 110, 116, 117, 120, 122, 123, 124 *top left and right, middle left, and bottom left and right*, 125 *top left and right, middle left, and bottom left and right*, 126, 132, 135, 138, 140 *bottom*, 144, 145, 146, 147 *bottom*, 148, 149, 151, 153, 155, 158-9, 161, 163, 171); Christa Hobmeier, Untermarchenbach (p. 131); Kreative-Pferdebilder/Lothar Krug, Oppenheim (p. 121); LL-Foto/Lars Lewandowski, Hilter a.T.W. (p. xviii *top right*); Birte Ostwald, Monsheim (pp. iii, v *top left*, vii, viii, xv, xvi *bottom left*, xviii *bottom right*, xx, 4 *top*, 5 *top*, 6, 9, 14, 16, 21, 32, 34, 35, 38, 40, 52, 56, 60, 61, 62, 64, 65, 68 *middle*, 69 *right*, 70, 73, 76 *bottom*, 83, 84, 88 *bottom middle and bottom*, 90, 93, 94-5, 99, 102, 104 *top*, 106, 107 *left*, 108 *top left and right, middle top and middle, bottom right*, 109 *top right and bottom left and right*, 112, 113, 115, 119, 124 *middle right*, 125 *middle right*, 128, 129, 136, 137, 143, 147 *top*, 150, 152, 166, 167, 170-1); Pat Parelli, USA (p. 100); Julia Rau, Mainz (pp. v *bottom left*, xii, 11 *left*); Jan Reumann, Bad Vilbel (p. 160); Silke Rottermann, Eberbach am Neckar (pp. 23 *right*, 29); Silvia Schröder/www.bestellung-reitsport-foto.de, Viersen (p. 162 *top*); Inge vogel, Langwedel (pp. 51, 133).

Cover design by RM Didier
Index by Andrea M. Jones (www.jonesliteraryservices.com)
Typeset in JAF Facit
Printed in Malaysia

10 9 8 7 6 5 4 3 2 1

Contents

Helios

Dino

Damon Jerome NRW

Le Noir

Dandelion

With Journal Entries:

Trouble-Free Interaction

The Cool Rider

Easygoing Through the Test

The Finale

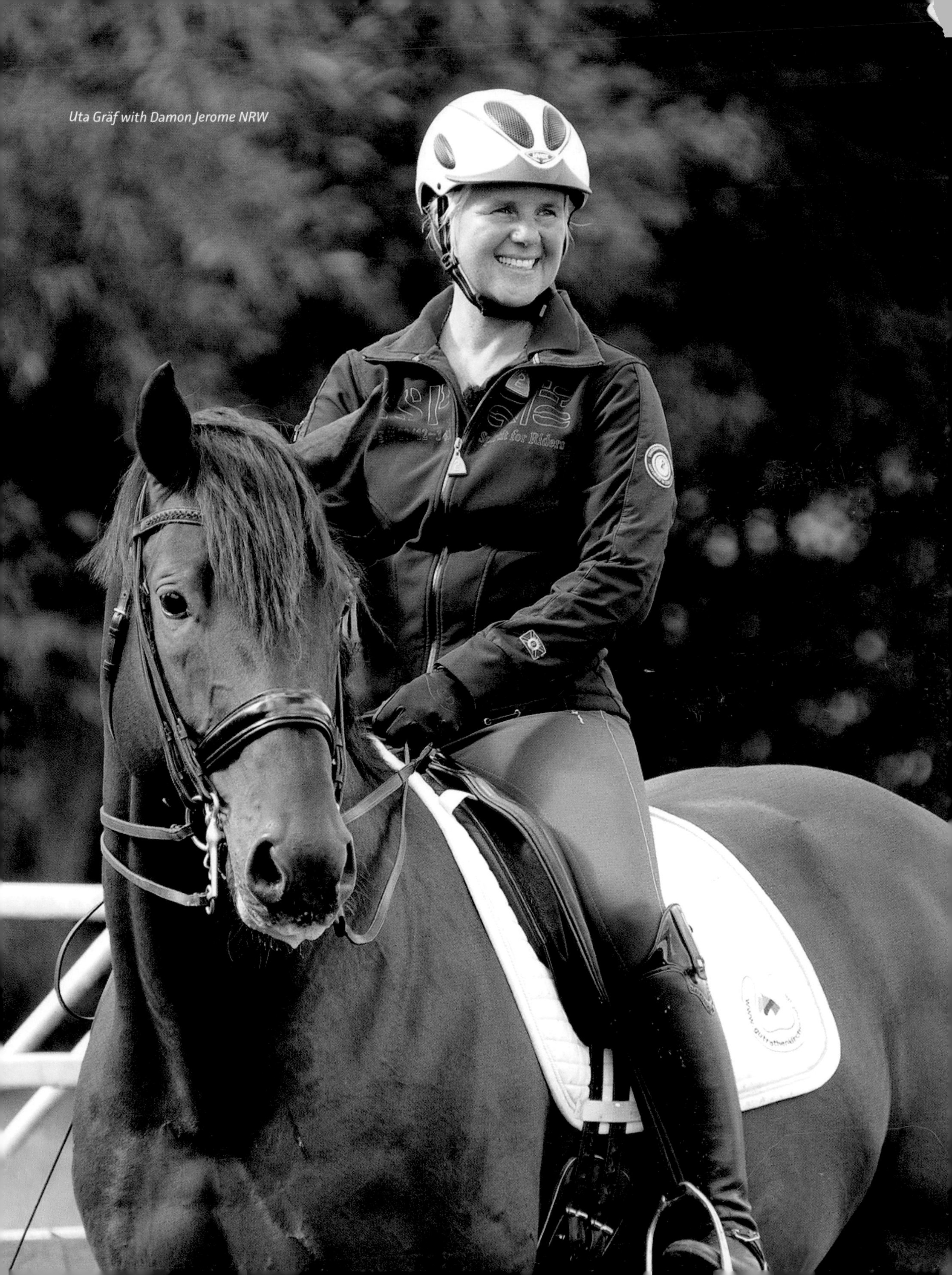

Uta Gräf with Damon Jerome NRW

Uta Gräf with Le Noir

Preface

Do you sometimes or maybe often feel exhausted after riding? Do you feel like you slog through without getting the results you want? Can you say your training rides and trail rides are soft and trouble-free? We want to take up these questions because the saying "less is more" is also true about riding! Our advice is: Have the courage to be lazy if you would like to achieve that special goal of riding with less effort and more effectiveness. You will find what we mean by that

as you read this book. Effortless riding doesn't mean simply sitting up there and resting. It is much more about balance, body coordination, and constantly refining the effectiveness of the aids. It also means working toward using less force when riding. By "trouble-free" riding we don't mean saving as much time as possible or minimizing effort in interacting with horses. Just the opposite: we work with the horses a great deal so that later we have less trouble when riding. My husband Stefan Schneider, for example, spends a lot of time working with the horses from the ground. This contact with the horses also gives us a lot of joy. We don't perceive it as burdensome. We know that later when riding we will benefit a great deal from it.

We have very much enjoyed receiving questions from riders of all disciplines and performance levels after the appearance of our first book in Germany, *Feines Reiten auf motivierten Pferden* ("Fine Riding on Motivated Horses"). We hope to address those questions here. We want to provide suggestions to all those riders who are missing softness in riding regardless of whether in competitive dressage, jumping, or on a riding vacation. Even a leisurely ride can become stressful, whether I am sitting on a "rocket" or my horse moves forward at the tempo of a shifting sand dune.

Many amateur riders only have one horse available to them and rarely have the opportunity to ride other ones to broaden their experience. For this reason, we think it will be helpful to give examples from our daily training (in the book's second half) after describing the basics (in the first part). We will be discussing various horses and how we have progressed with them. We hope these examples will give you the courage to believe in your own horse and give you ideas on how to proceed. Our examples demonstrate that you don't have to have a superstar to achieve something.

1 When we use the term "we" we mean both authors and the whole team at Gut Rothenkircherhof. Otherwise, Uta Gräf speaks using "I." Contributions from Friederike Heidenhof are so indicated.

2 We find that the text reads better when we only use the masculine form to refer to a horse.

As an equestrian professional, I have made effortless riding my top priority. It was clear to me quite early that I couldn't professionally ride five to eight horses a day if I was "hanging over the fence dripping" after the first ride. During my early riding instruction, my instructors focused not just on technique and expertise but also on the need to minimize effort when riding. I was lucky to have horses that taught me well in this regard—especially Le Noir!

Many riders have the impression that the horses have worked them rather than they have worked the horses. I was fortunate to have had instructors and horses that taught me to find a way to achieve the same or better results with less physical effort. It gives me joy to share this learning with my students and readers. The effortless riding that I strive for is not just to my own advantage, but ultimately benefits the horses. It is easy to understand that a rider who constantly rides with intense use of the body is not an especially pleasant partner on the back of the horse. More lightness, willingness to compromise, and the ability to feel the horse while riding contribute to the ability of the horse to enjoy being ridden so that he can unfold beneath us fresh and happy. Our motto "Drink Coffee in the Pirouette" is, naturally, a joke. But we use it to emphasize the principle of refinement of the aids. I frequently advise my students, "Make something happen, use the aids, be effective, so you can drink coffee." This isn't just at the High School level. It is true for every level of training and in all disciplines. But how do you reduce your physical exertion so that the effect is effortless? As a rider, how do I know my horse is going well? Should I ride a lazy horse with or without spurs? How do I follow your teaching when I have a horse that isn't so perfect?

To that end, we hope all you readers enjoy the book and find it rich in suggestions--without any effort!

Uta Gräf

Uta Gräf's Philosophy
by Friederike Heidenhof

Whenever I watch Uta Gräf, whether training at home or at a competition, it seems to me that she works her horse more effortlessly than I have ever seen elsewhere. It isn't just that she is scarcely sweating as she dismounts, you can almost feel the lightness when she trains. I noticed this again when we fitted Uta with a microphone for a number of videos of her riding. She was originally skeptical ("I don't like it when hearing someone puffing on a video"). But that skepticism was unfounded. Instead of the breathing noises she was concerned about, we heard a fully calm and relaxed voice.

Friederike Heidenhof and Uta Gräf

In addition to her riding program, Uta either jogs or does some other similar sport. This also suggests to me that Uta's energy expenditure while riding is fundamentally different from my own. I feel that I am at capacity with my one horse. Gradually, it became clearer what Uta meant when she admonished during a lesson "Prepare the horse well—then just drink coffee!" When I saw Uta for the first time riding Le Noir in a one-handed canter pirouette in the Grand Prix freestyle, it occurred to me that this principle actually works. I asked myself: what do I do that is different that I couldn't possibly think about drinking coffee when I am in the middle of a movement? And what is Uta doing differently when she can hold a cup while she rides a pirouette?

We have explored these questions together. I hope one day that it will mean I go riding and also to the gym. When I can do that, I will more likely understand effortless and effective riding. My horse will thank me. It isn't any fun for our horses when riders clamp, squirm, and bounce on their backs. The mottos, "Drink coffee in the pirouette," and "Scrape off the mud and ride the Grand Prix," are fundamental to the shared philosophy that Uta Gräf and her husband, Stefan Schneider, practice at Gut Rothenkircherhof. At the simplest level it means: horses can be allowed to be horses and still be successful in sport.

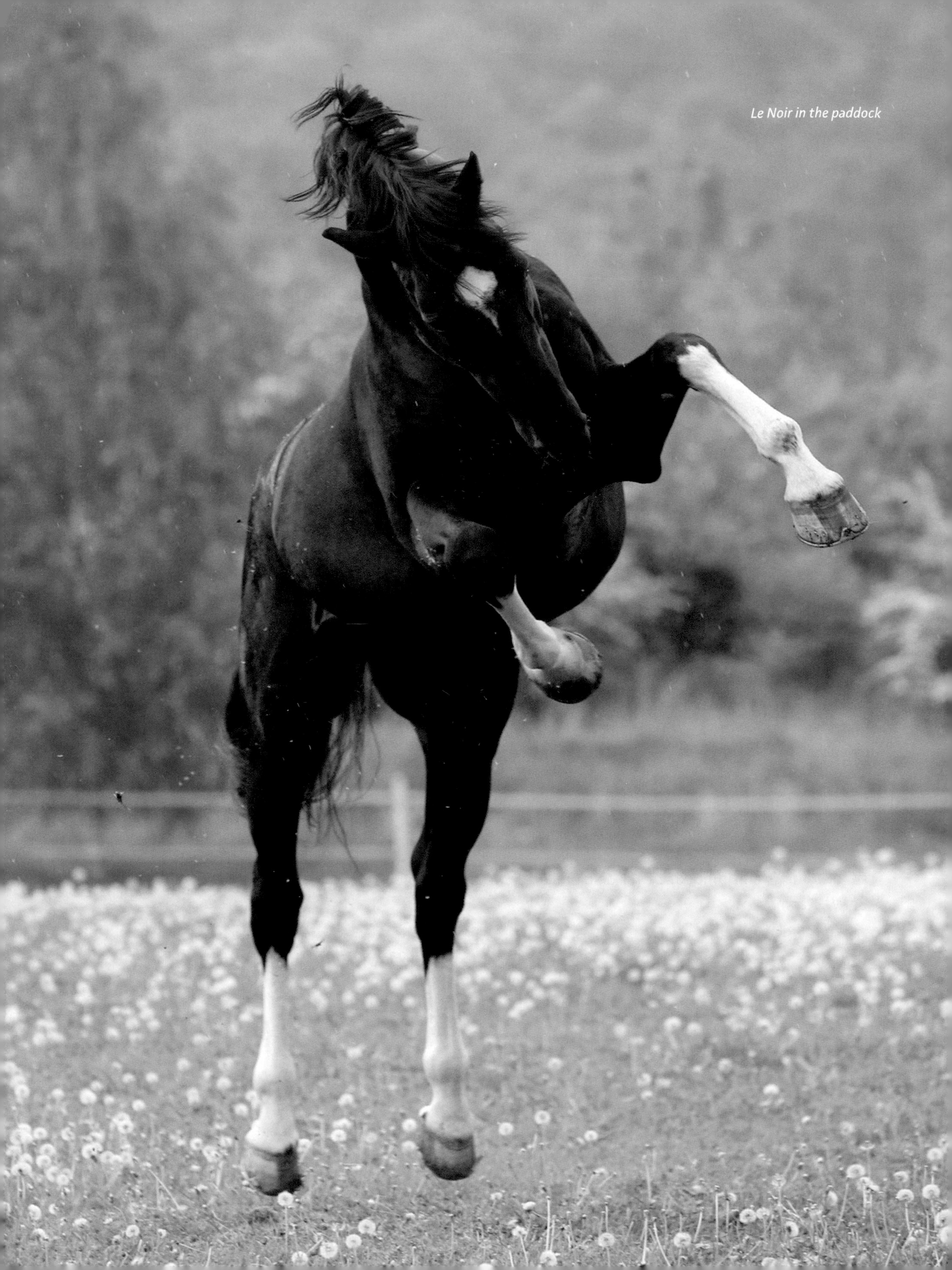
Le Noir in the paddock

A Principle for All Disciplines

Effortless riding is the result of a solid dressage education. It is fun for horse and rider.

We are convinced that basic training in dressage is a prerequisite for less stress and exertion in all riding disciplines. Many who use the word "dressage" mean the competitive discipline of the same name where riders in jackets or tailcoats and a top hat perform on well-trained sport horses. The layman connects the word "dressage" with an image of dogs, lions, or elephants in the circus performing entertaining acts to the applause of the public. That is exactly what it should *not* be.

Dressage doesn't mean the presentation of beautiful exercises. It encompasses all the gymnastic training that enables the horse to carry the rider's weight without sustaining long-term damage. Dressage doesn't have to end in competitive riding. Dressage training is fundamental for real riding in any discipline. It can lead to jumping, trail riding, or other disciplines such as working equitation, endurance, or Western riding.

We use the term "effortless riding" to mean that the horse can be ridden free from stress. If we riders understand that the horse was not designed by nature to bear weight on his back, we have the right view on the subject. Horses and their near relatives living in the wild do quite well without the additional load and don't need gymnastic training to stay fit. The rider's weight changes the horse's fundamental equilibrium because the "ensemble" of horse and rider in movement has a totally different dynamic. While it doesn't matter to the wild horse, donkey, or zebra if they are naturally a little crooked, an insufficiently trained horse can have significant problems caused by being crooked when carrying the rider's weight. If we ignore the crookedness and demand more physical activity than what the horse

Being ridden effortlessly: the horse is still fresh and full of life after the work and isn't dull. (Lexington)

does when living in the wild, we run a high risk of damage caused by one-sided loading of the body. You can think of it this way: if I, as a human being, were to spend a large part of my life with a heavy backpack, it would be reasonable to make some appointments with a physical therapist. The additional weight of the rider is somewhat like a hike with a backpack for the horse. Basic dressage work is an important contribution to maintaining the health of the horse, even when the leisure rider rides "only" a little. Without gymnastic training, the horse carries most of the weight on the forehand. When the horse is also crooked, most of the weight on the forehand is also carried more on one side (comparable to a hike with a heavy one-sided shoulder bag). It is our goal to make sure the horse is physically able to carry us riders effortlessly, so that he will later be able to accomplish more demanding work for us.

Dressage basic training also develops obedience, which is important at all levels of performance and for all disciplines. The goal of dressage training is to make the horse "through" and on the aids of the rider. The better I can manifest the steps of the training scale, the better the "throughness" of the horse at any level of training. The result is obedience, which is fundamental for safe riding whether in the woods, in the jumping arena, or in dressage. For this reason, it is not called the scale of dressage training but rather the "Training Scale." Rhythm, suppleness, contact, impulsion, and straightness are fundamental and necessary for any kind of riding. Even a minimal amount of collection is desirable because it helps to lighten the horse's forehand and make riding more pleasurable.

Summary: Dressage is not an end in itself. Regardless of what discipline or at what level of expertise you ride, basic dressage training has a solid place in every training program. It is important to remove physical or mental blocks and to keep the horse healthy despite the weight of the rider, and to enable him to succeed in further challenges. Dressage training also means making riding pleasant while maintaining the horse's motivation. Dressage is not just for the "perfect" horse, it is especially important for the not-so-perfect horse, too. Effortless riding—for rider and horse—is only possible with a basic dressage education.

Our Horses at Home

Because we are going to use our horses as examples of various training issues, we will introduce them next and show how our stars and supporting actors have progressed.

Let's begin with our "three wise men": Le Noir, Dandelion, and Damon Jerome NRW. Our three top horses have held their own in the upper levels and have climbed up in rank during the last two years. Along with their successes, they have blessed us and their owners with happiness. They enjoy being able to just be horses with the rest of the herd when they aren't in competition.

But, sometimes, it isn't all perfect in a horse's life. After a rather large competition, Le Noir didn't feel normal the first half of 2013. He didn't engage well and we had the feeling that he wasn't up to full work. Since we know Le Noir is generally eager to work, we gave him a long break from competition. At first, he simply chilled in the pasture, with maybe a trail ride and a few gymnastic exercises. Additionally, walking through water in the flooded automatic walker did him a lot of good. When we noticed that his eagerness had returned, we slowly increased the intensity of the training program until he was the same old guy again. Sure we had missed some great competitions, but we still had the joy of being with him every day at home and being able to whisper now and then in his ear, "You are, and always will be, the best!" Perhaps that is what helped him the most. The fall of the same year, after the break, he won his first Grand Prix—first time out.

Uta Gräf with Le Noir

Le Noir

Le Noir, our 14-year-old Holsteiner stallion (Leandro x Caletto I), recovered his full power and expression as well as the effortlessness of his motion.

His greatest successes so far have been winning the "Big Tour" in Wiesbaden and placing well in Aachen in 2012. In the same year he was on the long list for the Olympics and delighted his fans. Additionally, he is the sire of a whole string of promising foals. His owners Hans and Christiane Herzog are beyond happy with their Leo!

Damon Jerome was awarded the initials to his name NRW. As an approved Rhinelander stallion by Damon Hill (x Guy La Roche), he was only six years old when he won second at the World Championships and Reserve Champion of Germany. "DJ" is now nine, has gained a lot of strength, and can now control his extravagant gaits.

His rideability is as always "beyond words." He broke into the S level (Fourth Level/Prix St. Georges in U.S.) almost playfully. He had many wins at the S level in 2013 on the "Small Tour" in Wiesbaden, in Perl and placed well at the CHIO in Aachen. DJ also has picture-perfect foals. One of them has already been sold by his owner, Prof. Dr. Thomas Hitschold, as a promising young talent.

Dandelion

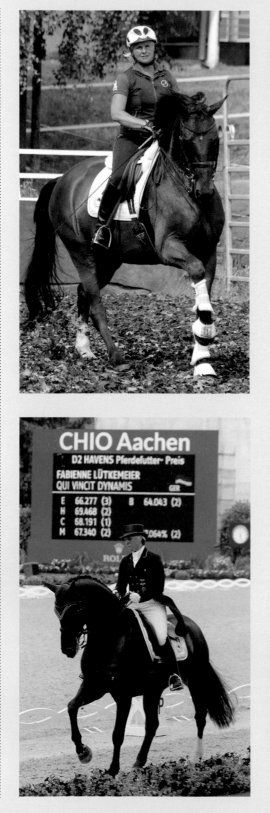

Dandelion, our 12-year-old gelding by De Niro (x Figaro) is the shooting star. From the M class (Third Level) to Grand Prix, from regional competitions to Aachen.

In 2013, "Dandy" got on the B list and was photographed with other international Donnerhall relatives. Nationally, in Germany, he won several Grand Prix competitions and captivated people with his powerful and expressive motion. At the CHIO in 2013, he placed among the top international horses; in Dortmund, he was second in the Grand Prix freestyle; and in Mannheim 2014, he won his first international Grand Prix Special. At home he is a lovable horse that is always a lot of fun, whether riding him or watching him tear around the paddock.

Later, we will be talking more about Escondido (Dino), that dear, all-around horse owned by co-author Friederike Heidenhof.

Helios is an eight-year-old gelding by Hibiskus. We will be telling his story more completely later in the book.

Also, we will talk in more detail about Le Noir and Damon Jerome NRW in the Journal of our horses: Le Noir as the "Successful Horse," and Damon Jerome NRW as a "Super Talent." In addition, we will report about our Newcomer, Dandelion, who has developed so well that he succeeded as he first stepped onto the international scene. All three are very powerful horses and each is a dream to ride in his own way—but more about that in our Journal.

Alongside these three "aces," we will discuss Helios as a horse of Normal Ability, and finally, Escondido, co-author Friederike Heidenhof's horse, as the "Not-So-Perfect Horse." Both have developed very well with a systematic gymnastic program.

Helios is the dream horse of his owner, Dr. Jutta Chirita, out of her mare Gloria. The goal: a rideable horse that her daughter could ride at the L level (Second Level). Today, we are practicing tempi changes and testing to see if he could one day learn piaffe and passage, as well. We will tell you more about his story later because there are many lessons to learn from his training: a) you don't have to be a super ace to give a lot of joy to the rider and b) talent hides in many horses that can blossom if they are given the time and carefully trained.

The same goes for Escondido (Dino), the eight-year-old average horse that fit into Friederike's limited budget. In his Journal, we describe in detail the training path of this dear horse who is so eager to learn. Despite his limitations, he brings joy every day.

Xinoca

The "small one," the Lusitano Xinoca, is big in the field of working equitation with Stefan. Working with his owner, Sandra Schneider-Rocker, Stefan has had the gray stallion under saddle for only three years and has already been successful at many competitions.

Finally, we are also enjoying riding the many horses that are already a success or simply lovely to ride at Rothenkircherhof.

We can't describe all our horses in the same detail as our Journal horses. Some of them will be used as further training examples. Among these are Durbridge and Raphaello, with whom I achieved my gold medal through multiple S wins. Also Duvalier who helped me move up to Grand Prix. Lexington, Le Charmeur Noir, Limbo, and Emmerson are young horses in training. We will meet them in the chapter about interacting with horses and starting them.

I would like to mention one thing that is very, very sad: Loffel, our donkey of many years, has moved. Since his job in life was to be a good companion to the owner's horse, he has followed him to another barn. Loffel is doing well at his new home. Before we humanize our animals, we should make it clear that *we* miss him, but that doesn't mean *he* misses us!

Xinoca, an eight-year-old Lusitano stallion out of by Queima-douro, is our working equitation star.

An Anecdote in Passing:

The editor of a large horse journal found it particularly regrettable that Loffel, who obviously has developed a certain level of notoriety, had to move: "Please let us know when you get another donkey at your place. We will immediately send out an announcement!"

Naturally, we appreciate the interest in the happenings at Gut Rothenkircherhof. But we laughed to ourselves as we imagined two announcements on the same page: Above: "XY has a new top horse in training that can be bought for a lot of money at an exclusive auction." And right below it: "Uta Graf has a new donkey…."

Effortless–But How?

The Independent Horse

The "Psycho" Horse

A fat tome we pulled off the bookcase at Friederike's parents is a rich source of psychological principles from days gone by: Wilhelm Blendinger's *Psychologie und Verhaltensweisen des Pferdes* ("Psychology and Behavior of the Horse"). He describes how the psychology of the horse affects his usefulness as a riding horse. He brings forth an important concept: both "work" and "sport" are foreign to the horse's nature.

As animals of the grasslands, the forefathers of our riding horses moved slowly around and followed the food. They only went faster when in flight. However, the desire to play can be freely expressed in motion for its own sake. In Blendinger's view, a foal's joy in playing can give an early indication of valuable characteristics that will develop later. Psychology experts put *sport* between *play* and *work*: sport differs from play in that it isn't about motion for its own sake and it differs from work in that it is not just being "useful." Without the participation of the human, sport is just as foreign as work, because both require a thought process. The human is the driving force for sport. It is true that all horse sports serve nothing more than to give joy of motion to a human that would not be possible without the help of the horse. There is no other feeling like sitting on a moving horse. In other words, without our interference, horses would play but never participate in a sport.

And now for the author's central discovery that can help us riders achieve an effortless lightness in everything that we do with horses: *Although sports are foreign to the horse because they require reflection, participating in a sport can be a middle ground between play and work for the horse—just as for the human—if he feels a certain joy in it. When you consider how a horse moves is similar in play, in sport, and in work, for example running, then the difference must be psychological. The body mechanics of running are the same*

In the pasture, our horses move powerfully and free...

... and relaxed at the walk (the herd at Gut Rothenkircherhof).

> "Relaxation is closely associated with the achievement of lightness!"
> — *Wilhelm Blendinger*

in all three cases. There is an essential difference in more or less obvious relaxation in the motion. True play is always done with relaxation and never with tense or cramped motion. Relaxation is closely connected to lightness.

According to Blendinger, young horses under saddle for the first time are confronted with work. He concluded several decades ago what has never been more important than today: "Young horses often move with tension when they must carry a rider for the first time. That is why loosening exercises are so important. Tense steps are frequent errors in dressage tests. 'Suppleness' and a soft 'connection' to the bit are signs of successful training."

Dressage training enables the horse to move with the same freedom and beauty as when he is free— even with the weight of the rider. Uta with Dandelion.

Excessive demands on a trained horse, or especially, a young horse, can lead to muscle tension. When the horses are insufficiently muscled up, they can't stand up to the work.

According to experts, *lightness* is a form of motion that most closely corresponds to the nature of the horse. When we are on a horse's back that is swinging and we notice that the lightness has not been lost, we are a step closer to effortless riding.

When we work for a long time against the horse's nature, we can cause neuroses that can be more or less intense and negatively affect the harmonious picture of fine riding. I exert much less energy in riding when my horse moves under me independently and I influence him minimally. The horse can move naturally and I can help him to reach his potential by interacting in the right way with his body and mind.

To achieve our goal of riding effortlessly and effectively, it is especially important to make training as playful as possible. Horses whose nervous system or body is overloaded because too much is demanded too soon, can actually become "psycho." Dressage horses that are pressured with exercises that are too difficult can become fearful and resistant, and jumpers can lose their joy in jumping when pushed to jump too high or attempt courses that are too difficult. According to Blendiger, the typical result of this in competition is rearing and refusing.

Blendinger incorporates the teachings of Sigmund Freud, in that the suppression of natural drives can lead to neuroticism as well as physical and mental disturbances. According to psychology experts, social contact is as important as playful and effortlessly progressive training and sufficient regular activity. Herd animals can only play and socialize in the company of their own kind. Blendinger says that the optimum number of participants for satisfaction of the play drive is around 20 animals. Perhaps it is no accident that we have about that many horses in our herd. We hadn't ever really thought about it.

Along with the need to play and have social contact, the need to belong and have a place in the herd has a special meaning for dressage training. According to Blendinger, this pecking-order drive is on display when the horse bears himself proudly with a raised head and arched neck and dances majestically. It is an essential goal of dressage to produce this carriage and motion.

The *character* of a horse, as we read further, is distinguished by a more or less strong will. Ultimately, it is a question of what a rider wants to do with a horse, that is, compete or trail ride. The purpose and also the character of the rider determines whether she is better off with a strong-willed horse or with one that is less self-confident. It would be a mistake to pass on a strong character for a sport horse because he is assumed to be more difficult to work with. Blendinger says the strength of will in a horse generally pairs with other characteristics, such as the need to move and a strong physical and mental constitution. The strong will of the

Our top young horses follow their need to play and be accepted (above, the geldings Feeling Good and Emmerson, and right, the stallion Lexington).

horse should not be overcome to slavish obedience, but rather developed to willing eagerness. Blendinger cites Xenophon: "A forced or misunderstood horse is never beautiful. It is just as if one forces a dancer to jump around by using whips and thorns. That is how a human makes a horse ugly rather than beautiful."

Bottom line: When we keep and train our horses so that the need to play, have social contact, have recognition in the herd, and character is not suppressed, we can reach an ideal point where our riding doesn't feel like "work" to the horse. Ultimately, our performance together can be perceived as effortless lightness.

Balance and Body Awareness for the Horse

We know what is necessary for trouble-free, effortless riding from a psychological stand-point. How can we translate this knowledge into practical riding—that is, playful riding, without it feeling like work? It works best when we allow our horses to balance themselves and develop their own body feel while being ridden. To do this we have to grant the horse a certain amount of independence consistent with Blendinger's concept of submission in "willing eagerness," which doesn't result in forced or learned

helplessness. Horses that live with a constant firing of aids, or that are trained locked in a frame, don't end up knowing anything about how they should use their own body. They lose the ability to balance themselves, and can't perform the desired exercises without the rider's constant interference. Lightness and effortlessness in movement are lost—along with beautiful expressiveness.

Ideally, the horse should be encouraged by us to find his own balance and to develop his own feeling for how to independently do an exercise, keep doing it, and have the balance to stop doing it. It isn't so bad if a horse in training loses his balance. It is much more important to quickly correct it rather than take away the possibility of the horse rebalancing himself by holding the aids too long. It is important to note that as the horse increases the load on the hindquarters through the training process, he automatically balances himself better and goes in better self-carriage.

The concept of balance is included in the Training Scale. Harry Boldt, German trainer and winner of multiple Olympic competitions, comments: *Balance is very important because it is the prerequisite for relaxation. I don't mean just balance of the body, but also in the head….This requires that the horse is always relaxed and straight….A horse in balance can always move better and more reliably in the required frame and in self-carriage. If a horse has difficulty with balance, he will try to compensate through crookedness. The rider needs to feel whether the horse is in balance under her or not…. Horses that are balanced swing through better and can more easily balance themselves in relative elevation….A well-balanced horse gives the rider more security regardless of the situation or the discipline.*

Letting the horse "chew the reins out of the hands" in all gaits while riding in a light seat encourages the development of balance in both horse and rider. Uta on Damon Jerome NRW and Helios.

Even a dressage horse should be trusted to canter over an uneven pasture without stumbling. Uta with Damon Jerome NRW.

Allow and Encourage Independence

Giving the horse his own balance has a lot to do with allowing him a certain level of independence. Naturally, "independence" doesn't mean the horse can decide for himself whether he will go by the judge's box or not. The horse must be obedient, stay on the rider's aids, and accept the human as the "boss." It is also important to make sure that we don't put horses in a straitjacket during our training out of which he can't move a millimeter forward or backward. This is true, not just for the purely physical aspect of training, but also the horse's mental state while being ridden. It is important for us to not discourage the horse. We try to achieve a mental and physical independence so that we can use our body less and less in riding.

The principle of "independence" begins with how you keep your horses. Those who are familiar with our methods know how important it is to us that our horses are allowed "to be horses." Our horse-care principles require maximum independence in natural environments with sufficient social contact, primarily in a large herd. Kept in this way, horses learn to take care of themselves over sticks and stones or on frozen ground. They train themselves to step carefully and balance to avoid injury and pain.

We don't want to take this away from the horses and overprotect them, even if they are valuable. We are convinced that dependent horses not only lose their "flash" and expression, but also the risk of injury is not less, but the opposite!

How can we animate our horses under saddle to be more independent within the previously described "guardrails"? For example, in the arena, many horses look for limits or connection. They often feel the fence is safe and try to maneuver to the outside track. But we want the energy of the horse to move from the hindquarters

Difficult terrain teaches balance and how to step carefully.

over his back to our hand in a fine connection. When the horse evades to the side, the energy is lost out to the side somewhere between the hindquarters and the shoulder. Riding on the second track helps to test the horse's balance and, thereby, encourages independence. We consciously avoid using the outside leg constantly to support the horse. The horse should hold the line by himself and only be restricted on one side when necessary. Just the opposite is true of our Grand Prix horse Dandelion. Because he loves to look around and is hard to keep on the track, we practice riding along the fence. The more he gets used to this the more independent I can allow him to be.

A second example: frequently riders tend to "hold" a horse in a gait by constantly and excessively driving every step or canter stride. In an extreme case, a horse breaks the gait when he isn't held in it with a lot of squeezing. This can work but it doesn't look light or free—and, in fact, it is not. Rider and horse expend too much energy, which means *work* for both instead of *play*.

How can it be otherwise? First, you have to get it clearly in your head that a certain independence for the horse is the way to the goal. It has a lot to do with trusting the horse, allowing him to work more or less alone under you. Here is a comparison to your professional life: If your boss didn't trust your work and constantly controlled and drove you, you would find the job to be exhausting instead of enjoyable. If he allowed you to be responsible for your work, you would be inspired rather than frustrated.

Along with trust, good preparation is important to the horse on the path to more independence. Let's take the canter as an example. Good preparation means asking for the canter when the horse is uphill and collected so he can carry the canter easily. Making the horse responsible means to take the aids off and see if the horse falls out of the gait. If he is about to stop on his own, drive him on until he canters independently, then take the aids off again. To get the feel for this, it is helpful to ride on the longe so you can experience how it feels when the horse "independently" moves under you, without you having to take much action. This also teaches a rider to trust the big movement of a talented young horse so that she doesn't inadvertently "cut off" the canter by pulling him back too much out of fear, which dampens the horse's independence and joy in moving.

I can grant the horse a little bit of independence by giving him the choice in certain situations. For example, if I want to activate the hind leg with trot-walk-trot transitions and my horse keeps responding with a canter, it is sometimes smarter to choose another strategy. Repeated corrections can create an argument or frustration. Instead, I allow the faster gait, then move into shoulder-fore at the canter, which causes him to carry more weight on the hindquarters. This exercise works just as well as a powerful trot transition—his choice! Repeat it a few times and 90 percent of the time, the trot transition is easy to get. All exercises embody the same principle: give the horse the opportunity to find his own solutions independently, let the horse feel good about using other ways to get to the same goal. If you want to try something new as a rider, you have to forget about perfection and expressiveness at first. Many riders don't feel sufficiently free from the judgment of others. So here is our tip: if you are self-conscious in front of other riders, practice when no one is around!

Being able to pulse the aids is important to more independence and effortlessness. In the scope of classical dressage training, the aids are to be given briefly at the right time then removed once the horse gives the right response. Your leg stays in "hair" contact with the horse without being fully removed. Your hand needs to have a constant vibrating contact without the rein looping. If the horse doesn't react appropriately (the aid didn't come "through") you should pulse the aid again with a little more energy, but immediately get quiet when the horse has responded correctly.

Le Noir—Journal of a Success Story

Expert on the Subject of "Pulsing the Aids"

BACKGROUND: Let me say up front that Le Noir, his owners the Herzogs, and me coming together has changed all our lives. I never thought I would say such a thing about a horse—especially one that I thought had already achieved what he was capable of. Le Noir came to us for training as an eight-year-old and was on the way from dressage Level L to M. Because he was raised and trained at a location far away from the Herzog family, they didn't have frequent contact with him. Le Noir didn't have the chance to win their hearts, as he has done today. We are all thankful that he wasn't sold halfway along, which could have easily happened.

CHALLENGES: The biggest challenge was to get to know Le Noir. At the beginning he was quick to clearly show us what he liked and what he didn't. Communication was difficult to establish because Le Noir overreacted sometimes when my aids weren't sensitive enough. He did not like it at all when I neglected to leave him in peace even though what he had already given me was good enough. He taught me to lighten up as a rider. What is so special about Le Noir is his sensitivity, coupled with energy, eagerness, and an enormous capacity for work. I had to learn to be clever enough to get along with him and to strengthen these qualities. The concepts of "independence" and "pulsing the aids" were critical.

Training program for an eight-year-old: It was easy for our stallion to make the jump from Levels L to M (Second to Third Level), learning the new lessons like flying changes of lead at the canter and half-pass. It was a challenge to keep his eagerness within positive limits because he tended to offer the exercises in advance of the aids and take off. To avoid a battle and frustrating Le Noir in the independence he wanted to have, I instituted a lot of change to the program and took care to not do an exercise on the same spot. For example, I would ride a diagonal with flying changes then one without. Or, one time I'd take up the reins and break to a trot then next time take up the reins and *not* break to a trot, instead letting the reins go long. In this way, I could avoid extinguishing his independence, but have him understand that only I as the rider knew what was coming next.

RESULT: At eight years old, I entered Le Noir in two M classes where we placed fourth in one and didn't place in the other. After that we spent a few months at home and practiced more. We were thrilled to read the judge's comments: "Super horse!" None of us expected at that point that Le Noir would one day develop into an international success.

Le Noir taught Uta his definition of "effortless," which she tries to achieve with other horses.

Le Noir is a perfect example of how important it is to think about the character of your horse and motivate him to think with you. Le Noir has been and is a good teacher for me. If we had suppressed his eagerness and his independence, he probably would not have developed into such a successful horse. When a horse seems too independent at first, for example, by taking over in the flying changes, it is important not to get irritated but rather to turn the disadvantage into an advantage. When that happens, and training is progressed as cleverly as the horse is intelligent, you end up working with a partner that is ready to give *all* for the rider. If not, it can end in frustration and lack of motivation.

Independence obviously doesn't mean to just let the horse run. He must stay collected and "through" and on the aids of the rider. This enables him to find his own balance that makes effortless riding possible. The horse develops brilliance and his natural potential movement unfolds. It simply feels better if horses are happy, relaxed, and you can feel that they enjoy the work. Ideally, you can find the middle path between the play drive and work. Today, I benefit from Le Noir responding so sensitively. In the Grand Prix, it is an unbelievable feeling to just think about changing and Le Noir knows exactly what I want—but waits anyway. I was able to take the concept of effortless riding to a completely different dimension with him. From him I have learned how much I can lighten my aids. Without him we would never have come up with the idea of *drinking coffee in the pirouette* as a slogan for our book. Not every horse is as sensitive as Le Noir, but I now know where the bar for me is set on the topic of effortlessness. I can take that intention to my other horses and try to get closer to the ideal.

Let the Horse Think Things Through!

by Ingrid Klimke

Escada's ears are perked: one turns back to the rider then forward again, in full concentration on the next obstacle. Ingrid Klimke is wearing a helmet camera as she rides Escada as one of four horses through the demanding cross-country course in Luhmühlen. As we watched the film we held our breath. We watched in fascination as the horse attacked one difficult obstacle after another: angled walls, extremely tight in-and-out combinations, jumps into unknown depths, into water and over the proverbial stick and stone. It seems like Ingrid had more often to tell the horse what *not* to jump. The rider is obviously dependent on the horse thinking things through and making his own decisions about getting round the course. For this reason, we asked Ingrid to write a guest section giving you her philosophy. We believe this fundamental idea is important for dressage and trail riding, but in cross-country it is especially obvious and critical.

Ingrid Klimke: As a rider, I carry all the responsibility for myself and my horse. I am the one that decided we should do this work together. Nevertheless, during the ride, I give about 50 percent of the responsibility for the execution of the individual jobs to my horse. As the rider, I indicate the direction and the line, and regulate the tempo. I let the horse handle the jump. I don't know exactly what happens at the jump because the horse must analyze the situation in milliseconds and decide how to jump it. Consequently, as the rider I can't dictate whether he should get to the obstacle in four or five canter strides. The horse can best decide that himself. I trust that he will independently take the initiative.

This principle also applies to dressage and you can learn a lot from it. For a horse to remain motivated over the long haul, he has to be able to think things through.

Ingrid Klimke with Butts Abraxxas at the London Olympic Games, 2012, and with Dresden Mann at the CHIO in Aachen, 2013.

> "At the end of the day, a horse's trust is more important than his ability!" — *Ingrid Klimke*

My father Reiner Klimke always told us how ugly performances look when the horses reel off the exercises in pure "wooden" obedience without any thought, which means that I start the exercise and the horse finishes it! I allow my horse a certain degree of freedom. I "ask for something," give the direction, and wait for the horse to respond. If there is no reaction, I will aid more distinctly and award any reaction—any tendency in the right direction. For example, if I want to get a horse used to riding through water, I say, "We will now go into the water together." That we ride through the water is not up for discussion and I am clear about that. However, he can decide *how* he goes through the water, at first. He can walk in, he can jump in and out, or he can go through in zigzags, or whatever. The main thing is *through* the water. Later, we will find the best and most efficient way together.

It is the same for me in dressage. When a horse is learning flying changes and he leaps afterward, that isn't so bad for I have dictated a job to do (canter-lead changes without a change of gait) and the horse found a solution. It isn't yet perfect, but he can't know that yet. I effusively reward the response and let the horse relax. Later, I work on collection and energy until the change is correct according to our expectations. I do the same thing with cross-country jumping. I say to the horse "I want to go over it with you somehow." The horse searches for an answer and I praise him regardless of whether he jumps over it or flies over it like a helicopter.

Every step in the right direction deserves praise. I give this degree of freedom to the horse because I see it as one of the most important prerequisites for success, but more importantly for enjoying the task together. There is no fun in riding stressed out and tense horses, which has nothing to do with the "art of riding." I take it in stride that a horse might look at something during the dressage test, or maybe fall apart in the pirouette. That can happen, but I wouldn't do it any other way. Not at the price of having to spend my whole life "squeezing" and "pressing" with my legs. The horse loses his self-confidence when you stress or pressure him after a mistake, and that can destroy the joy and harmony of dressage, while in cross-country, it would be in a disaster. If I had to run a cross-country course—like Luhmühlen—carrying the horse around, I would be completely exhausted by the end.

I much prefer getting in balance with the horse and noticing if we both feel good and are enjoying the course. Horse and rider must have enough joy and strength left for the last passage-piaffe-passage series in the Grand Prix test. Consequently, I am not the absolute dictator, but rather show the way and encourage joy and self-confidence. Trust is more important than the ability of the horse!

Ingrid Klimke's example helps us to know that we can rely on our horses even in borderline situations when we don't incapacitate them. Below are a few exercises that can help our horses develop better balance and independence.

Practical Exercises for Balance and Independence

The Classical Way

■ **To improve balance:** Ride on the second track or on the centerline and don't let the horse drift to the outside. Riding shoulder-in on the second track instead of the first track is a better test of whether the hindquarters fall out.

■ **To improve independence**—shoulder-in, for example:

- Maintain the positioning and bend out of the corner.
- Sit down, adjust the reins, and make him more active.
- Move sideways to the right angle and let him flow independently.
- Reduce the aids.
- If he loses swing, leave the lateral movement and activate the horse riding a curved line.

Give This a Try

■ **To improve independence:** Pulse the driving aids. Ride him to the hand, making sure not to get in the way of the fluidity of the movement. Save energy for the next exercise, don't squeeze or clamp.

■ **To improve independence:** Test the canter by consciously taking away the driving aids in order to see if the horse will continue cantering with very little aid. If he falls apart, start cantering again, drive in pulses before he breaks, and take the aids away again.

■ **To improve balance:** Leg-yield on the diagonal, then straight, without wavering.

■ **To improve balance:** Ride rectangles away from the wall.

■ **Balance exercises:** Ride in-and-out jump combinations in a light seat. Allow the horse to chew the reins out of the hand in trot and canter. In these exercises, horse and rider learn to bring their own body under control.

■ **Seat exercises on the longe are not taboo for advanced riders!** You have to be able to balance yourself and sit supple enough, so the horse can move freely and find his own balance.

Damon Jerome NRW takes the corner without losing his balance. Uta uses the light seat in order to school good balance.

What I Have Learned from Uta Gräf

by Friederike Heidenhof

Above all, I have learned that allowing the horse to find his own balance is a question of trust. Until now, I had never internalized the idea of allowing the horse a certain amount of independence. Perhaps it was due to the riding accident I had in my youth, after which it was hard for me to trust a horse. I tended to want to "frame" the horse and control him. From Uta, I have learned that I can let the horse work independently beneath me if I trust he won't run off at any moment or put me in a fix. Letting the horse chew the reins out of the hand so he can balance with his neck requires as much trust as does stopping my bad habit of clamping my thighs on the horse. To avoid this, I imagine that my horse is on the longe line and that he can't bolt. This helps me leave it to chance. I have learned that a rider can be careful without having to constantly squeeze the horse. When the horse-care conditions are right and the training program sufficiently varied, I can build more trust with my horse as a rider so I don't feel the need to over-control him and squeeze him into a frame. Little by little, I am getting the feeling of having a balanced horse under me. I can better feel if the exercise we are trying to do is easier and the whole ride is more effortless. It's probably the same for my horse….

Crookedness

In horses, the concepts of independence and balance are closely associated with the concept of crookedness. When a horse is crooked and carries more weight on the forehand, he isn't sufficiently balanced. Since we now know how important balance is for effortless riding, it makes sense to carefully examine the natural crookedness of the horse. Crookedness and the change in the horse's whole dynamic caused by carrying a rider can make it constant work to bring the horse into correct carriage. Straightening a horse is a life-long job for the rider. However, for more effortless riding, it is more important to accomplish it through appropriate gymnastics rather than the constant use of the aids. Straightening is not an isolated point on the training scale that you can work on once and then forget forever. Richard Hinrichs remarked: "Straight is the line of greatest resistance. That is also true for riding!"

> "Straight is the line of greatest resistance.
> That is also true for riding…." — *Richard Hinrichs*

There are many theories about the cause of crookedness. The most common one is that a foal lies to one side in the mother's body, suggesting that crookedness is already present. Every foal has his "favorite side" from which he will spring into canter. Horse psychologist Blendinger maintains that crookedness is the result of the horse's handedness (similar to right-hand and left-handed in humans) rather than the cause. He maintains that many horses prefer to go to the left and can do everything more easily in that direction. To even him out, gymnastics to the right are necessary to straighten the horse. According to Blendinger, many right-handed riders have a left-hand twist that inhibits the necessary bending to the right. Right-handed people tend to ride more easily to the left. This works against straightening the horse and also burdens the forehand on one side. It is important for riding horses to be worked in such a way that they can almost forget their natural born preference (Blendinger). Note: Training should always begin on the side that is easier for the horse. Gymnastic exercises for the horse should never be overdone on his more difficult side nor exaggerated. It doesn't help to "torture" the horse with one-sided gymnastics. He will not be motivated—just overwhelmed. It is far better to work at it slowly.

The shoulder-fore is a good exercise for straightening the horse. I take the aids away to make sure I am not driving constantly, and I wait. If the horse loses the shoulder-fore, I simply guide him back to shoulder-fore and take the aids off again. The horse must learn to balance himself. It seems to me that riders begin with the more difficult side in many cases. This leads very early to "fights" and then there

Lateral work is important for straightening. Without straightness, there is no balance, and without balance there can be no effortless riding! Uta on Damon Jerome NRW.

can be no thought of effortless riding. Consequently, it is better to start every exercise in the easier direction then go to the more difficult side.

I understand gymnastics for the horse much better from having a back problem of my own. In my experience, appropriate exercises can help you get your mobility back little by little without having to drive or torture yourself too much. Training a horse is similar to rehabilitation. When the gymnastic exercise makes things better, keep going. When things get worse, it is better to take a step back. That assumes, of course, that I as a rider am sensitive enough to tell early enough if the horse is getting better or worse. I don't want to ride around on a problem and make it worse. If I am not sure, it makes sense to get a trainer involved.

Why have we made this detailed journey into horse physiology? It's very simple. The continual correction of crookedness is the prerequisite for the horse to find his own balance so that he can do the exercises asked of him without the rider having to "carry" him or constantly correct him. If you don't have straightness, riding is difficult. Because the horse has been crooked for so long, most have to slowly rebuild the musculature to fit the work. It can take a while to straighten a horse. But having him straight makes it possible for you to ultimately give the horse a certain degree of independence during an exercise so he can balance himself.

It is clear that dressage is not an end in itself, but rather the means to the end, which is to build a harmonious and fluid unit out of horse and rider. Having a straight horse is not just important for dressage. To correctly approach a jump, it is necessary for the horse's shoulders to be on the same axis as his hindquarters. When the horse is crooked, a lot of energy escapes to the side and he has a harder time with the jump. A refusal is often caused by a horse not being straight enough. On this point, Martin Plewa, leader of the Westfalian riding and driving school in Münster says in *"Training Paradox"* (Reiter Revue 9/2013): "When a horse canters crookedly, he also jumps crookedly. This makes combinations and distances difficult because the distance between jumps is larger due to the crookedness." Successful jumpers use exercises like half-pass in their dressage work to straighten the horse.

Summary: Encouraging the horse's balance and body feel is fundamentally important for further correct training. Straightening is an important prerequisite for this and makes effortless riding possible.

Practical Exercises for Straightening a Horse

The Classical Way

- **Walk down the centerline toward the mirror and make sure the front end and hindquarters of the horse are on the same track.**

- **Check your own seat for crookedness and correct yourself.**

- **Ride on curved lines and keep the hindquarters from falling out and the horse from falling to the outside through the shoulder.**

- **Shoulder-in or travers:**
  - Bend the horse around the inside leg and drive him into both hands.
  - When finishing the exercise bring the forehand in front of the hindquarters.
  - Adjust the contact away from the bracing side (stiff side) to the lighter (hollow) side.
  - Release the aids as soon as the horse is straight.

- **Do transitions from one gait to another and also changes of tempo within the gait to strengthen both sides of the body.**

Give This a Try

- **Ride half the arena:** Ride through the corner in shoulder-fore. After every corner, straighten the horse on the track and ride him evenly into both hands.

- **To test:** Ride voltes and check that the horse keeps the front end and the back end on the same track.

- Think about a little shoulder-fore in every corner and turn: Start curved lines in shoulder-fore.

- Ride frequently on the second track and on the centerline to check if the horse is staying straight.

- Ride shoulder-fore along the centerline, changing from side to side. The hindquarters should stay on the centerline and not weave.

- Leg-yield or shoulder-in for only 5 meters, then straight, then 5 more meters of leg-yield or shoulder-in.

Exercises for Balance, Straightness and Independence

Goal	Exercise	Result
Encourage balance	Seat exercises on the longe for your own balance. Ride without stirrups or without a saddle if not dangerous.	Notice what it feels like when the horse moves independently.
	Ride frequently on the second track or the quarterline.	The wall is not there to hold the horse up. He maintains his own balance.
	Canter in a light seat cross-country or in the arena.	The horse moves without being excessively held together by the rider.
	Allow the horse to chew the reins out of your hands at the trot and canter on curved lines. Don't let the horse fall apart or bolt.	The horse continues to work with light aids. He learns to balance himself.
	Cavalletti work, in-and-out jump combinations. For advanced riders, drop the reins on the neck and stretch your arms out to the side.	The horse learns to find the best way for himself. The rider trains her own balance.
	Ride a trail course: serpentines around cones, barrels, and other obstacles.	Rapid changes of direction improve balance.
	Stop the exercise as soon as swing, position, or bend are lost. If the half-pass deteriorates, ride shoulder-fore, then go back to half-pass.	The horse learns to keep his balance himself.
Straighten	If the horse swings the hindquarters to the inside: shoulder-fore or shoulder-in. If the hindquarters drift to the outside: travers.	Both sides are strengthened. This promotes lateral balance.
	Frequently change the canter lead when riding outside (right lead canter, left lead canter). Change lead through rising trot.	This keeps the horse from using only the softer side. Both sides are evenly loaded and worked.
Independence	Consciously remove the aids during a lesson or exercise. If the horse breaks, start over until the horse maintains the exercise with little help.	It becomes clear if the horse is working independently or has to be "carried" through the lesson.
	Often ride in a stretch position in all gaits while keeping the weight on the hindquarters.	Prevents getting too closed in the throatlatch and encourages a friendly, yielding hand.

Eager, but Not Rushing

Our Journal horse Escondido teaches us that we must work with and study each horse as an individual—especially as regards tempo. It can sometimes be tricky to find the right way to go. To be able to ride effortlessly, the horse must be energetic under the rider. He should not have to be constantly asked again and again, nor should he run off.

Dino—Journal of a Not-So-Perfect Horse (1)

Eight Years Old: One Step Back, Two Steps Forward

by Friederike Heidenhof

Dino

BACKGROUND: Escondido ("Dino") is an average horse with basic gaits that are part good and part limited. He is a "not-so-perfect" horse, as his not-so-perfect-rider calls him, taken from the book *Dressage for the Not-So-Perfect Horse* by Janet Foy. He is by the Hanoverian stallion Escudo I, who sires good jumping horses. Dino was trained by the previous owner as a dressage horse and was only jumped a little. Until I bought him as an eight-year-old, he lived with his family. The first year went pretty well. Dino is especially drawn to people and has a deep trust for "his" human. He developed strength and power, but wasn't challenged enough. Due to lack of time, he was put up for sale. It was a good fit because I wanted a horse that was sweet and healthy and liked to work with his rider.

CHALLENGES: At the beginning, Dino wasn't always effortless to ride. Sometimes, he was strong and frequently went against the hand. He lacked "throughness." Positioning and bending were also difficult. The trot didn't swing. The canter was frequently flat and four-beating. Dino was restricted in the walk and it's still a problem today. Nevertheless, training has always been fun even when it was a lot of trouble to get everything right. It has taken a lot of work to improve his problem areas.

EIGHT-YEAR-OLD TRAINING PROGRAM: With Christina Dahl, a very good rider in our barn, we took a step back in training. We began with basic work and delayed working on movements.

TIPS FROM UTA GRÄF: Uta helped me to understand that it wouldn't make any sense to focus too soon on showing. We spent about a year on throughness: transitions, circles, and tempo changes. This reduced his tendency to rush in the trot and canter without killing his natural forward energy and eagerness. To improve the walk, we ended almost every dressage training session with a ride out to relax him.

RESULT: Dino was eager to learn from the beginning. But he had a tendency to go against the hand in every halt and to rush. With time, his throughness improved and we could maintain better rhythm and tempo. The whole thing was no trouble—at least for me—but not so correct.

Since Dino is a horse that tends to rush, we carefully begin every training session by slowing the tempo somewhat. With a different horse it is better to ride forward. In any case, it is important for the rider to pay attention from the beginning and maintain tempo and rhythm. There is a fine line between control and constant control. Ideally, I should have the feeling that I *could* influence the horse if necessary, but don't *have* to all the time. The horse shouldn't set the tempo by himself. The rider chooses the tempo where the horse feels the most comfortable. The art is in letting a horse work eagerly, but not hurriedly. Even a rushing horse must be activated so that he moves with more swing. This can be achieved, for example, with lateral movements that naturally elevate and collect the horse using driving aids without unconsciously increasing the effect of the hand. In lateral movements, the horse is animated to step with more activity. Admittedly, this is difficult.

> "The horse should not set the tempo by himself. The rider chooses a tempo where the horse feels most comfortable."
>
> — *Uta Gräf*

In dressage, setting the rhythm and tempo is a prerequisite for precise riding of movements. In jumping and cross-country riding, it is the rhythm and the riding of distances. Good rhythm and an appropriate tempo protect against one-sided or over-use injuries in cross-country and in trail riding. True loss of control can even be dangerous.

While Dino tends to run off at the trot and to canter flat, many horses are sluggish and seem lazy to the rider. Often, they are merely dulled by constant driving. Both are evasions to stepping powerfully with true activity and swing. They don't do it because they are against us or because they fundamentally don't have any desire to work with us.

They are simply looking for the simplest way. Obviously, you must exclude health issues and also, check: saddle, bridle, teeth, shoes, weight (too fat or too thin), weather, change in hair coat. If nothing is rubbing or pinching, try to solve the problem with clever training.

Most good-natured horses can be motivated to more activity. They normally enjoy moving and we riders are the rate-limiting factor. A horse that seems lazy—the opposite of Dino—usually has had his desire to go forward destroyed by a rider using too much hand to get through the poll. This is an important key point. The horse has lost his energy, so most riders begin to drive continually. This makes riding exhausting. Riding exercises, movements, or jumps becomes a tough business.

It is important for the rider to give the horse energy by riding more to the hand and avoiding using a backward acting hand. She should move with the horse and carry herself without constant effort and use pulsing driving aids. In their book *Dressage with Kyra*, Kyra Kyrklund and Jytte Lemkow use the picture of a scooter that goes on its own a distance once it is started. The scooter is pushed when it loses momentum. That's how it should feel to sit on an energetic horse. Connection and riding through the poll come from the forward energy. It is often the right thing to put horses that want to invert (go above the bit) a little deeper with sensitivity and ride them forward over the back to a soft hand. Many riders make the mistake of thinking "head down" and, thereby, destroy the horse's natural desire to move forward.

It is our goal to have the horse in front of the leg. He should immediately react to sensitive driving aids by going more forward and stepping with more power. If he

The leg lies quietly against the horse. Uta has taken her driving aid away after the desired reaction from Damon Jerome NRW.

Le Noir steps actively without hurrying. Uta with Le Noir.

> "Imagine a scooter that continues to move forward for a way after it has been shoved. It is pushed again when it loses impulsion. This is how it feels to sit on an active horse."
>
> — *Kyra Kyrklund and Jytte Lemkow*

does not, the aids are to be applied again briefly with more energy. Richard Hinrichs has a wise saying about this: **"Clarity of the aids is more important than invisibility."** Thinking in this way, it is not bad if a horse canters off or leaps a little forward. If your horse reacts a little too strongly, be happy about it and let him move forward. Don't work backward. That can be interpreted as punishment by the horse. Every reaction forward should be rewarded, especially with a reduction in aids. If the horse is moving as you want, relax! Don't fall in the trap of always wanting to help your horse just so he stays moving.

> "Clarity of the aids is more important than invisibility."
>
> — *Richard Hinrichs*

As long as you aren't using any special aid, your leg should lie against the horse with completely relaxed muscles. Whip and spur aids should also not be used continually. Many riders unknowingly stick the horse on the side with the spur with every trot step, especially in posting trot. The spur should only be used to refine the aids! This can only happen when they are used only when needed and not used at all for long stretches of time. After a successful forward aid, you should test whether a lighter aid now gets the same response from your horse. If not, you should aid again with more energy. When the horse responds well to your aids, you are another step further along the way to effortless riding, and your horse will definitely feel better about you as a rider.

Every training session should end with a positive experience. This makes it easier at the next training session or at a show. It is a dream when a horse is so active that he will give you everything during a test. Ideally, we shouldn't lose activity, impulsion, or expression either when we introduce an exercise or during its performance.

Working with swing and an active hind leg ultimately leads to the piaffe and passage. Uta with Le Noir.

Even while on a relaxed ride out, an energetic and through horse is a dream. Uta on Le Noir.

Practical Exercises to Make the Horse Active

The Classical Way

- ■ Practice in hand letting the horse move willingly and energetically next to you.
- ■ While walking at the beginning of the training session, concentrate on activity and follow the nodding movement with the hand, but don't let the horse rush.
- ■ Drive in pulses rather than squeezing all the time:
  - · Increase the aid if there is no response.
  - · Immediately reduce the aid when the horse shows a response.
  - · Consciously relax the legs and "let them hang."
- ■ Ride transitions and demand a prompt start:
  - · From trot to walk or halt, with or without rein-back.
  - · Trot out of the halt and ride walk-trot transitions.
- ■ To prevent rushing: ride on curved lines and in lateral movements.
  - · Regulate rhythm and tempo without putting the brakes on, meaning without working backward with the hand. Add in the driving aids.

Give This a Try

- ■ In walk-trot-walk transitions, go into the trot immediately, activating the hind leg.
- ■ When picking up a canter, move really forward so that the forward impulse doesn't become half-hearted.
- ■ In transitions of gait and changes of tempo take control back now and then but watch that you don't get stuck in constant aiding.
- ■ Help from the ground:
  - · Assistant points the whip toward the hindquarters of the horse.
  - · Activate the horse while consciously relaxing yourself without gripping.
  - · Notice what it is like when the horse moves forward on his own.
  - · Catch the forward impulse in your vibrating hand. Offer a sensitive connection.
- ■ Train outside of arenas: walk, trot, and canter, with hills if possible:
  - · Going uphill the horse must use the hindquarters more powerfully.
  - · You can also practice movements out in the field without losing activity.
  - · The horse frequently has more "go" and carries himself forward.
- ■ Motivational training program with lots of variety without overwhelming the horse.
- ■ Take a look at how you are caring for your horse and make changes:
  - · Horse should be able to move freely about to increase activity.
  - · Conditioning is improved.
- ■ There is a positive effect on the mental outlook.
  - · Seat exercises on the longe and gymnastics: Practice supple sitting without disturbing the horse to increase his joy in going.
  - · This is also for advanced and competitive riders.

Poll Up—Nose in Front of the Vertical

For our next Journal horse, Damon Jerome NRW, it was important to keep his forehead in front of the vertical in his training. He was naturally elevated, very light in the hand, and gave me a good feeling as a rider. Without looking at the mirror now and then, or getting advised by my trainer or a colleague, I might have let him get behind the vertical many times. Damon Jerome NRW has not only extraordinary gaits but also the mind of a very talented child. Using him as an example, we would like to show that even with such a talented horse, success doesn't automatically fall in your lap, even though everything so far has been fairly easy for him. You must be very careful not to skip a single step in the training. "Grass doesn't grow faster if you pull on it," is a common saying. Balance, rhythm, tempo, and connection were never a problem for Damon Jerome NRW. But even a "super talent" needs his time. We would like to show you where the dangers could have been that we had to work around so that we wouldn't have trouble later with such a highly talented horse.

Damon Jerome NRW ("DJ")—Journal of a Super Talent (1)

Four to Six Years: Direct the Energy Down the Right Road

BACKGROUND: Damon Jerome NRW is now a nine-year-old stallion by Damon Hill (x Guy La Roche). Willi Schneider, the breeder, sent him to us for training as a four-year-old. I had ridden him before during a switch-rider test. We were glad that his new owner, Professor Thomas Hitschold, was able to acquire him shortly thereafter.

CHALLENGES: At the beginning, it was important to not take advantage of Damon Jerome's natural elevation too early or for too long. We were concerned about him bracing his back, which would have limited his potential ability to move. From the beginning, DJ was very secure and constant in the contact and felt like a six-year-old horse. But be careful! If you get too comfortable with this as a rider and accept the elevation that a horse offers too early, it can lead to problems later. True self-carriage requires muscle and power from the hindquarters. Otherwise, too much is expected of the horse. The horse can get tense and the poll is no longer the highest point. This is usually accompanied by a throatlatch that is too narrow (behind the bit) and incorrect muscling. We had to keep all this in mind during DJ's training program in order to preserve his lightness, effortlessness, and elasticity. We had to keep his energy and willingness to work directed in the right way. For example, he has a huge ground-covering, energetic canter.

Damon Jerome NRW

It required a little courage to ride this huge movement on a young stallion still more energetically forward while always keeping the nose in front of the vertical. But it was necessary so that the horse could jump through with the hindquarters as far forward as possible. To ride this horse in too controlled a manner would have been fundamentally wrong and could have taken away his love of moving, motivation, and his natural looseness. Beginning poorly would have led to a difficult time working together later.

TRAINING PROGRAM: I rode DJ with changing levels of elevation. When he wanted to carry himself "up and in," I changed the contact to put him in a stretching position. Over the course of the training, I increased the loading of the hindquarters and animated him to self-carriage in stages by riding many curved lines and changes of tempo. I also added in leg-yields, and lateral movements such as shoulder-fore and shoulder–in. I rewarded every bit of progress by letting him chew the reins out of my hands to travel in a stretching position while riding him energetically forward. Meanwhile, my husband Stefan Schneider took him through a course of groundwork that made riding much easier for me. Just as with highly talented children, it has been and always is important to change things up a lot in DJ's training program so that he stays motivated and doesn't shut down emotionally.

RESULT: Whatever young horse test or demonstration we rode, he scored 8s, 9s, and even 10s for all three gaits. At six, DJ was vice-champion of Germany and vice world champion of young dressage horses and was the most winning six-year-old dressage horse in Germany. I enjoy every day I am able to ride such a horse. It isn't possible to translate into words what effortless riding means on a horse like DJ.

It was important to assure that DJ would keep his nose in front of the vertical, because that comes from enough drive from behind forward to the hand. Good connection makes it possible to ride on the aids with a fine contact to the horse's mouth. The path to effortless riding involves how you train a horse to a certain neck carriage. This is not just for dressage, but also important for jumping. A horse that reaches to the hand can also reach over the jump and push himself off powerfully. In leisure riding, consistent contact with a fine connection is important for enjoying the ride without any annoying rolling over (going too deep), inverting (going above the bit), going against the hand, or pulling. The uphill tendency in good connection with elastic activity of the back comes from the hind legs stepping well underneath and more weight being shifted to the hind end. If the croup lowers, you have elevation. "Poll up—nose in front" is no end in itself: the throatlatch stays open, the horse steps to the bit, the back swings, and the hind legs can swing as far as possible through (at the trot) as well as jump well under (at the canter).

Many riders have already achieved a lot with their horses, but the poll is rarely the highest point and the nose is rarely in front of the vertical. I ask myself why this is so and try to remember what it was like as I began riding. In my environment, "nose in front of the vertical" was a noble goal and something we left for the impractical textbooks. Still, today I have the impression that most riders know that it should be different but have actually no idea how to make it happen. Or they think "poll high" is something that is only relevant for dressage tests. It can also be that the willingness is there but the feel from above is misleading. From on top of the horse it can look like the poll is the highest point while it looks very different from below.

Damon Jerome NRW at canter in good self-carriage with the poll the highest point and the nose in front of the vertical.

When he starts chewing the reins out of my hands at the trot, DJ stretches to the hand and his nose stays in front of the vertical.

A quick look in the mirror can tell you that the horse's mouth is pointing in the direction of his chest and that his throatlatch is too narrow (behind the vertical). Some riders might have trouble getting the horse to go "over the back" when the poll is up. Most learn as riding students that it is important to ride the horse on the bit. That is also correct, but many riders understand this to mean that the head of the horse must be "down somehow." It seems normal to have the horse with an arched neck and the nose behind the vertical. Some riders fear that their horse will get above the bit as soon as they let go of this position. Or, it is pure habit.

Ingrid Klimke said this on the subject: "Basically, I always have an image in my head of my father on Ahlerich at the 1984 Olympic Games in Los Angeles. Ahlerich's poll is the highest point, the nose is distinctly in front of the vertical. Today, many would probably say that he isn't on the bit. But he is, because he is relatively elevated. The hind leg steps far under the center of gravity, the back is carrying, and the rider swings in the middle. The horse is clearly in front of the driving aids."

If a rider has ever experienced the feeling of correct connection, he will understand that "poll up" is an important step to effortless riding and that it can make the life of horse and rider much easier if they can manage to keep the nose in front of the vertical with the horse still coming over the back and through the poll. It must all come together. "Nose forward" alone isn't sufficient to work a horse well. Ideally, the horse also takes more weight on the hindquarters, carries himself, steps to the rider's soft hand, and yields in the poll. His mouth seeks the forward-thinking hand and carries the nose in front of the vertical. From this position, the horse must be able to go into a stretching position and let the neck fall at any time. Devoting enough time and attention to this aspect of training has paid off for DJ.

In conclusion, our goal of effortless riding is for the horse to be straight and balanced, active behind and traveling over the back through the poll to the hand, "bouncing" off the bit and in beautiful self-carriage. He develops swing and athletic movement similar to what is seen when he's moving free without the rider.

The poll is the highest point and the nose is distinctly in front of the vertical. Dr. Reiner Klimke on Ahlerich on the way to winning the Gold Medal in Los Angeles, 1984.

Right? If yes, then I think it is clearly important for the rider to know how it feels when the horse is "good" in this sense. We have already mentioned looking in the mirror, but videos and the feedback of a trainer also help. We need to mention here that riding is difficult. It is not always easy to achieve the ideal just as we would like. We should guard against hastily shaking a finger at others who haven't yet been able, regardless of why, to keep their horses' noses in front of the vertical. The horse I'm riding isn't always in front of the vertical. This happens most often, for example, when I am first showing the horse the way to the hand in the stretch or when I am working on a new movement. That isn't so bad, but it is important to me to always be watching and to correct it right away and never let the horse get stuck in this position for a long time. Consequently, I allow the horse to chew the reins out of the hand often—in trot as well as canter—during training as well as in the warm up arena at a show. I pay attention that the nose is truly ahead of the vertical in the stretch position as well and that the horse doesn't roll over (go too deep behind the vertical).

When we asked the international dressage judge and trainer Angelika Fromming if she would read the manuscript of our first book, she immediately agreed. It was important for us to hear her critical assessment and suggestions for any changes. She suggested that we change out a photo of Le Noir although it really was a beautiful picture. At the moment of the photo, Le Noir's poll was just below the highest point. In the manuscript, we found a correction: horse ears drawn on the picture of Le Noir a few centimeters above his own ears. A thick arrow on the edge of the manuscript bore the writing "better like this!" We were amused by the hint.

Now when I teach I only have to say "Attention, the ears!" and everyone knows the poll of the horse has just dropped and needs to be corrected right away.

Some horses are so soft in the poll that they can get behind the vertical quickly. While I like such horses, many riders prefer a horse with a tighter poll. I ride horses with a soft poll by frequently changing their elevation and with many transitions and changes of tempo.

The "Ears Picture"
Better like this!

Even at the A level of dressage, it is important to strive to ride with the poll as the highest point and the nose in front of the vertical. Paula Flumann with Dino.

Even in a working equitation trail course, the poll stays up and the nose in front when riding around obstacles. Stefan Schneider with Xinoca.

This encourages better connection so I can allow the nose to be in front of the vertical. I ride transitions with horses that are stiff in the poll and tend to go against the hand by using the last steps before the halt to catch the energy in a vibrating hand without blocking the forward energy. The horse can push off the bit and come into a better self-carriage. This is exactly the moment when the horse sets the hind leg and takes more weight on the hindquarters. At this time, he is able to become light on the hand. I can then create a fine connection to the hand and allow the nose to be more in front. I then try to preserve this frame with a more open throatlatch as I trot or canter off.

I would like to mention again how helpful it is when a rider gets the chance to feel what it is like to ride an active horse in correct connection and self-carriage. The horse can direct his gaze ahead and I as the rider have the feeling that the whole dynamic and energy of the motion can flow freely forward, while I still have control over rhythm and tempo. It is easy to steer a horse that is moving in good self-carriage and connection even through difficult movements. There is more impulsion and the front legs can move in a more beautiful way. His activity is not blocked and he doesn't require constant driving aids. That is the art of riding that I experience as effortless. As a rider, I can also help average horses blossom. With many horses, there is the danger of blocking the natural energy and motion when they get behind the vertical. It is especially important for the horse of average talent that he be supported so that his available potential is maximized by making the ride as effortless as possible.

"Jumping is dressage with obstacles in the way!" The jumper has to be able to see and go to the next jump—likewise with a high poll and the nose in front of the vertical. (CHIO Aachen, 2013)

Good connection is especially important so that they can be easily controlled in the hitch. (CHIO Aachen, 2013)

Practical Exercises for Improving Connection

The Classical Way

- To check for self-carriage, stretch the hands out briefly in trot and canter (*überstreichen*).
- Assure that you know where the poll is:
- Ask a trainer, other riders, look in the mirror, or take videos.
- Notice how the right position feels.
- Improve connection and self-carriage through transitions and changes of tempo. Feel how the pushing and carrying power improves.
- Make sure that "head down" isn't the first thing you think about:
- Correct the occasional inversion by riding forward without a backward action of the hand.

Give This a Try

- Drive the horse into sometimes more, sometimes less weight in the hand to test your ability to influence him.
- Allow the horse to chew the reins out of your hands at the trot or canter to check to see if the self-carriage is correct:
- If the horse immediately drops his neck, all is okay.
- Watch that the nose stays in front of the vertical and that the throatlatch stays open.
- If it takes forever until the horse stretches, something isn't right.
- Take the horse up again, ride him forward to the hand and in front of your leg and let him chew the reins out of your hands again.
- In training, change the elevation often: more elevation, then less elevation—like a Level A dressage horse (First Level); then forward-downward, then with more elevation again.

Friederike and Dino in a lesson with Uta.

Dino—Journal of a Not-So-Perfect Horse (2)

Nine Years Old: The Difficult Jump from Levels L to M (Second to Third Level)

by Friederike Heidenhof

It was necessary for Dino to move now and then to Gut Rothenkircherhof since Uta and I started our book and video projects.

CHALLENGES: Problems with correct contact (poll up—nose in front) affect throughness. It makes it harder to ride him to the hand because Dino likes to go against the hand. The collected canter is still flat and rushing and lacks jump if Dino isn't carrying enough weight on the hindquarters. In the half-pass we lose rhythm and swing, and it is hard to maintain positioning and bend.

NINE-YEAR-OLD TRAINING PROGRAM: Uta emphasized improvement in purity of the gaits and throughness. Transitions and changes of tempo develop power for increased weight-bearing behind which improves self-carriage and collection. These were important prerequisites on the way to more lightness and using more sensitive aids.

To improve the jump in the canter and increase weight-bearing behind, we used pirouette preparatory work, consisting of going in and out of travers and shoulder-fore on smaller circles. We had already included individual flying changes in the exercise program. Christina Dahl helped me a great deal with them at home. Dino learns very quickly and is always motivated by them. It is especially good that he doesn't get excited during the difficult exercises, if he is given enough breaks.

TIPS FROM UTA GRÄF: At first, I had the tendency to work against stiffness in the jaw by constantly trying to have control over the poll. Dino was frequently behind the vertical, causing his back to stiffen and making it difficult for the hindquarters to swing through elastically. Uta corrected this and watched that I kept the poll up and the nose in front of the vertical. On this subject, I told Uta that several years before when I was able to ride her competition horse Durbridge I had an "aha" experience. I felt what it is like when a horse pushes from behind through the body and steps to both hands "up through the poll" and immediately yields in the poll. I wanted to try to have this feeling on Dino. Previously, riding behind the vertical was so natural for me that I considered it completely normal.

To my astonishment, Uta told me that years before, she too had a realization about riding her horses in front of the vertical. She also was focused on the poll with the nose behind the vertical and hadn't yet learned what it meant to have a horse in front of her. Now I often hear Uta in lessons: "That wasn't bad--now you must let the nose be more in front." She added the sobering and a little exaggerated addition: "about half-a-meter!" She encouraged me to leave the horse alone as soon as he was good. We practiced transitions and circles without Dino diving down. We also worked on relaxed swinging of the hindquarters because he tended to show undesirable hovering-trot steps instead of moving in active collection.

RESULT: The tough parts improved through regular training. However, at a show my horse and I were still too nervous and I couldn't take Dino's good abilities into the test with me. In his training, I hold to the saying, "The tortoise can tell more about the path than the hare." Dino now gives me a fantastic feeling under saddle since he has gotten stronger and his gaits have gotten more pure and impulsive. In the current stage of our training, I am getting an idea of what it can feel like to ride with less exertion.

Dino

Uta with Le Noir

Effortless–
But How?

Allow the Horse to Work Under You

Less Is More

We are getting much closer to our motto "Drink coffee while in the pirouette," which we apply in a figurative sense to all our exercises or movements. We have already written about what we need: balance, activity, connection, and self-carriage. Now it comes down to us as riders to consciously sit still and let the horse work under us. Naturally, I am influencing my horse all the time. But we want to achieve distinctly effortless riding with as little exertion as possible. This goal is not just for dressage—even though we talk about pirouettes as an example in our motto. Even in leisure riding or on the jumping course, it is important to find an effortless partnership.

Here is how to make the exercise effortless: prepare the horse well then let the half-pass "flow." Uta with Dandelion.

We have already described an important aspect of the horse's balance and activity. I try consciously to not constantly "help" the horse. If I keep aiding him to go at the desired tempo, I dull the horse and wear myself out. I concentrate on letting the horse work under me and immediately correct now and then, as necessary. For me to relax, the horse must stay on the aids. I only engage when I notice that something is getting worse. To notice this, I must, as the rider, be able to stop constantly aiding the horse and test if my horse stays on the aids when I reduce the aids to a minimum. It is important to have a good ability to feel the ride in order to be able to correct my horse at the right time.

For example: Let's say you are sitting the trot and have encouraged your horse to a more active step and swing. You feel the impulsion in your hand and your horse is going in good connection and self-carriage. It would be wrong to keep aiding him when you are satisfied with this success. It is more correct to take the aids away to test whether the horse continues in an impulsive trot in good connection and self-carriage giving you a good feeling without your constant help. My tip: Consciously remove the aids and relax into your training session. Trust that your horse will stay "good" even when you aren't continually asking.

When you are about to lose that "good" feeling, you must return to being a helper or aid-giver. At the beginning, two steps of relaxation are better than none. We have to pay in advance for the lightness we want or we can never expect our horse to move like a featherlight ballerina. Pressure creates counterpressure—that is a new idea. I don't want to constantly push my horse, nor do I want to actively drive him forward through the poll, or hold him in a certain position or bend. I prefer to work toward my horse maintaining the position we have achieved until I ask for something else.

Notice when it is good:
- The horse is relaxed, active and willing.
- The poll is the highest point.
- The nose is in front of the vertical.
- The horse pushes from the hindquarters over the back through the poll to the hand.
- The horse is in front of the aids.

Leave the horse alone:
- Sit relaxed and loose into the movement and let him take you.
- Take away the driving aids.
- Let him step to your soft yielding hand.
- Praise him with your voice.

Aid effectively:
- Increase pulsing driving aids.
- Catch the energy with a vibrating hand, then offer a soft steady connection.
- Stop the exercise, if necessary, to reestablish position and bend, swing, and collection.
- Continue with the lesson or exercise.

Notice when it is getting bad:
- The horse is not in front of the aids, activity/connection are lost, the horse dives down or doesn't elevate.
- Loading of the hindquarters and self-carriage are insufficient.
- Position and bend are lost.
- The rhythm is not pure or tension develops and the swing is lost.

This graphic describes the principle again in individual steps. The maxim to not do all the work as the rider and constantly help the horse is especially impactful when the dressage exercise or the requirements of a jumping course are more difficult. In these cases, the horse must increase the loading of the hindquarters, which requires the horse to expend a lot of energy. Many riders tend to use their entire body weight, literally burrowing into the saddle and bringing their upper body behind the vertical, in order to shove the horse from behind. Richard Hinrichs addressed this at one of his seminars with the poignant words, "Everything is moving, except the horse!" It does no good; you only get tired. You need to reserve energy for the next exercises or jumps that come faster one after the other with higher tests of greater difficulty. It is better to aid briefly then allow the horse independently to work beneath you. I can effectively practice the increased loading of the hindquarters, for example, with canter-walk-canter transitions and by reducing circle size.

I always have it in my head that my horse is responsible for carrying more weight behind. I only think about what I want to achieve. If my horse drops to trot in a transition from canter to walk something was wrong with my preparation. I must be more effective (using pulsed driving), then sit relaxed and allow the transition to happen—without squeezing. Then check to see if it was well done, praise the horse, leave him alone, then repeat. It is counterproductive to throw your upper body in the canter "jump" before the halt using all your energy in the saddle with seat and legs cramping, dragging the horse into the transition. An average horse weighs about 1100 pounds. This is way too much mass to work against. It *must* work differently. Otherwise riding is just too hard!

The motto, *drink coffee in the pirouette,* is a little exaggerated in that I obviously can't completely remove all aids. I just want to make the principle clear and encourage you to always work toward a minimal aid so that riding can be more effortless and ultimately more harmonious.

Practical Exercises for Riding with Less Exertion

The Classical Way

■ Ride canter-walk-canter transitions:

- Try to do a specific number (for example, 10 canter strides and 10 walk steps), and repeat a few times. This increases concentration. Keep minimizing the aids.

■ If forward energy is lost, increase the tempo. When this is easy to do, come to a walk with little use of your body.

Give This a Try

■ Test what the horse offers without much effort from you (for example, regarding tempo):

- Aid effectively so he knows what you expect of him.
- Reward his response and consciously reduce the aids.

■ Remove the driving aids, post the trot, let him chew the reins out of the hand, and test to see if the horse still goes actively forward, and see how much the aids can be reduced without the horse stopping.

■ Prepare the horse well for exercises such as lateral movements or riding curved lines, then let it flow without excessive constant application of the aids:

- Break off the exercise when you have lost the activity, prepare him with increased forward energy and let it flow again.

Le Noir—Journal of a Success

Nine Years Old: The Penny Has Dropped

The first two competitions at the M class (Third Level) weren't very successful, so we decided to train more at home. We needed to become a better rider-horse pair.

CHALLENGES: Like many stallions, Le Noir didn't like it when I used too much leg. I was never sure whether I was going to be able to use my aids without upsetting or frightening him. So I asked myself: can I so refine my aids so that Le Noir accepts them?

TRAINING PROGRAM FOR A NINE-YEAR-OLD: We continued to work on half-passes and changes and started including some S movements in with our M exercises. I consciously focused on letting the horse work under me and to make my presence on his back as pleasant as possible. I understood that I must not push him around. He must work independently. Le Noir wants to do everything right, but he also wants to be treated well. He also wants my full concentration when we practice something difficult. Even a short interruption by the trainer can cause him to lose focus if I am not with him even for a moment.

Uta with Le Noir in their first Level S class (Fourth Level/Prix St. Georges).

RESULT: During the short break from competitions, the penny suddenly dropped. Le Noir and I rode many M and S wins. From then on everything has been easy for him.

At the beginning I wasn't actually sure that Le Noir was the right horse for me although he had always been a beautiful stallion with an A plus character and perfect to deal with. I am thankful that my husband Stefan encouraged me to keep trying to find a way to a better relationship. Le Noir taught me along the way. It is a special ability to feel something before it happens. It is almost like telepathy, and it is possible in riding. As we described in the "four-step circle" (see p. 36), ideally I give the aid before something goes wrong. "Realize, analyze, react" must occur in seconds. This makes effortless riding possible.

A Question of Timing
by Christoph Hess

In order to ride with less exertion, correct timing of the aids is especially important. If the rider doesn't give the aid at the right moment, the aid might not be effective and you won't get what you want. This leads quickly to the horse being confused. Balance, suppleness, and good coordination in the rider are important for good timing of the aids. When the rider sits relaxed and independent of the hand, he can act quickly enough with weight, leg, and hand in the right moment. Correct timing of the aids comes largely from experience and becomes unconscious coordination. To perfect the little things in the pursuit of effortless riding, it can be helpful to work on the timing of the aids. With a little practice, fine adjustments become second nature and the rider will use her "body language" at the right time, unconsciously. When the timing is right, everything between horse and rider runs smoothly. There is almost no disruption causing confusion. Some riders naturally have a good feel for the right timing, but you can learn it.

This is why it is so important to work on a supple seat and to practice having the horse in front of you, on the aids, and with good connection. It can also be helpful to ask your riding teacher to coach you from the ground as to when to give the aids until you get a good feel for it. In order not to be just a little off in timing, it is important to ride looking forward and always think about the next thing. Instead of "I want to stop trotting," it is better to think "I want to start walking." By thinking about walking, I can automatically aid my horse so that his first step is pure in rhythm, and relaxed. Correct timing comes from good preparation: the horse is collected, attentive, and waits for the aid, which the rider ideally only has to think about.

Christoph Hess, FN—Training Ambassador

Strategy of the Soft Voice

On the way to making our aids as sensitive and subtle as possible while still being effective, our voices can be very useful. I use my voice as an additional level of communication with the horse from the beginning. When I sit in the saddle, I use my voice just like I would when working with a horse from the ground or when longeing. Using the voice from the saddle has the effect, above all, of relaxing the rider and allowing her to concentrate better. I use my voice to support the riding aids. If horse and rider are a good team, the voice can help in special situations, for example, when the horse is excited and hot. Calming words can be enormously helpful to defuse a situation. Here also, less is more, because it wouldn't help the horse to jabber on and on from

Dino turns an ear to the side and reacts in the moment of the transition to his rider's soft voice.

above. The sparing but precise use of the voice is another helpful component of more effortless riding. It begins with gaining the trust of the horse with a calm voice.

Everyone knows the long drawn-out vowels in "goooood." The horse would understand "stuuuuuupppiiiid" to mean the same thing if it is said in the same calming voice and connected with the pleasant feeling of a relaxed rider. It depends on the tone of voice and the loudness. The meaning of the spoken word doesn't matter. Horses have excellent ears. They hear everything easily, even a whisper.

For example, Friederike has had good experiences using her voice in transitions. Dino knows the voice command "waaalk" from longeing. Friederike can also use it from the saddle to get a harmonious canter-walk-canter transition without using her hands a lot. She prepares the transition well in advance by increasing collection and weight on the hindquarters in the canter. Then she uses her whispering voice exactly in the moment when the transition should follow. After a few times she needed nothing more than a soft "wa…." The voice can be softer and more subtle until you don't use it anymore and the transition is still good.

I also use my voice unconsciously. Spectators have told me after a test they were amused that I told Le Noir, "It doesn't matter!" after a mistake in a movement. Obviously, this could be heard at the end of the arena but I didn't remember it. Since I say this often during training, I must have said these words during the test. "It doesn't matter" helps me not to stop at mistakes and to give the horse confidence to simply try the next movement eagerly.

Learn from the Para-Equestrians

As the riding trainer for the handicapped in Rheinland-Pfalz, I frequently see how much can be done with hardly any aids as in the cases of people like Britta Näpel and Hannelore Brenner, whose legs are partially or completely useless. Angelika Trabert has had to get along from birth with almost no leg usage at all, since her legs are extremely short. She began riding as a child. Luckily, she had parents who supported this decision despite their concerns, although they themselves were not riders. All three of these riders have been decorated with WM and/or Olympic medals in Para-Equestrianism. They have also been successful up to M and S levels in sanctioned competitions. How is this possible? Their success is due most of all to talent, patience, desire, and the will to achieve despite a handicap.

I think we can learn a lot from the para-equestrians. Whoever has the opportunity to watch such a competition live should definitely do so.

This has positively moved me and changed my viewpoint and attitude toward my own riding (and life) in many ways. While riders without a handicap are immediately in the saddle, for para-equestrians it's a "three-act play" before they can even get started.

Angelika Trabert: "It's Ability!"
About Her Life and Riding with a Handicap

Dr. Angelika Trabert on Ariva-Avanti.

I was born with my handicap, so I don't know any other way. Perhaps that makes it a little easier to feel "normal" even without normal legs. It wasn't easy for my parents when I wanted to ride, especially since they had no experience with horses. But it was the best thing that could have happened to me because the horse is the best compensatory assistant there is. He accepts us as we are. Most two-leggeds could learn a lot from this. I can successfully challenge myself in regular as well as handicapped horse sports, but also get to explore new terrain-- in the mountains or on the beach! "It's ability, not disability, that counts!" is my motto. There are many opportunities. One must only take advantage of them. So, for example, I work part of the year as an anesthesiologist with a surgery team in Africa, I go skiing, have tried diving, and I ride. I love the challenge. The word "impossible" is one of the greatest motivators for finding solutions.

The difficulty in riding is that my center of gravity is relatively high and I can rapidly end up sitting in the sand next to the horse if he jumps to the side, for example. The most important thing for me is to be balanced. I must pay close attention to this and feel myself precisely in sync with the motion of the horse. Lateral movements are a special challenge—for me as well as for the horse. They require perfect, sensitive timing in the use of the aids because I must send the horse sideways as well as forward with the aids that are left to me (especially weight and my whips). I have to stay in balance and my seat and the whips must be sufficient to send the horse sideways.

Often, I would love to have a leg to help me, but, ultimately, it works okay with a sensitively trained horse. I have to trust that my horse won't leave me hanging as soon as I soften the aids. Perhaps this is an advantage over the non-handicapped riders because I can't squeeze with my legs or continuously help the horse at every stride. The horse has to take me with him in his motion. The exercises must "flow," because I can't help with every walk, trot, or canter stride.

From the wheelchair to the horse. At home, she can almost do it by herself. At a show, Dr. Angelika Trabert needs a two-legged assistant.

Upper right: Even in the warm-up arena you can see that Ariva-Avanti responds to the very fine aids of her rider. If you didn't already know it, you would scarcely notice that Angelika is riding without legs.

Angelika Trabert asks Uta her opinion about her ride. Both are very pleased.

So how do the para-equestrians do it? Initially, the leg function must be replaced with aids such as whips carried on one side or both sides. The whips are used just as a non-handicapped rider uses her legs: precisely when necessary. First of all, you can't clamp on with a whip like you can with legs. Secondly, the para-equestrians only have the whips and no ability to use a spur when the horse doesn't respond. Since the riders with limited leg function don't have another "arrow in the quiver," they must be very careful not to "use up" the whip aid and make the horse numb to it.

Angelika, Hannelore, and Britta have internalized in their riding how important it is to let the horse work under you. They have been able to do this because their trainers work with the principles of classical dressage. It is especially important that the fundamentals are there: a balanced, straight horse that actively moves forward with impulsion and responds to sensitive aids. Para-equestrians are the living example with their successes (even at sanctioned competitions). It works! Riding without effort isn't just "nice to have" for them, but a "must have"!

Britta Näpel: "Despite It!"

Unlike Angelika Trabert, Britta Näpel was not born handicapped. She completed training as a professional groom and worked in a horse business until one fateful day when she used insecticide in a stall that caused her paralysis. When it was clear that half her body was permanently paralyzed, it was also clear that she could no longer pursue her career. But she didn't give up and also didn't give up on riding.

Britta Näpel: With riding, I had to come to terms with what would work and not be held back by what might not work. For example, because of my handicap I can't post the trot. Naturally, this has consequences for my horse in the warm up and also for my own relaxation. For many years I had done otherwise, which might have made the transition more difficult for me than for Angelika who has never known it. On the whole,

Britta Näpel on Aquilina and Uta in Mannheim.

I have learned a lot from my limitations. I now ride with much less physical effort, simply because it isn't possible to do so much "action." With Uta, I have learned that little body effort is necessary to reach the goal. I can solve the posting trot problem, for example, with longeing. And, I can do some stretching exercises on the ground before riding to loosen up. When on the horse, I am careful not to use up the aids that are still available to me. I try constantly to relax myself and let the horse work independently beneath me. It is especially important to keep my horse in front of the leg so that I can ride him harmoniously with fine aids. And it works!

Durbridge, Rob Romeo, and Invisible Touch are the horses that came from Uta Gräf and Stefan Schneider at the right time. With them, I won the World Championship and Vice-European Championship in para-equestrianism. All of the horses were sensitive in their own way and have given me what Uta calls, "endorphins for the rest of the day." Other horses that I now ride benefit from the lightness I felt, and they forgive the unnatural aids. The horse has to learn to ignore a spasm shooting through my legs and not canter off. That the horses are able to do this shows me once again that we aren't working with sport machines but with sport partners!

(Britta Näpel)

Hannelore Brenner with "Women of the World."

Hannelore Brenner: "Don't Defeat Yourself!"

For Hanne Brenner, riding is part fate and part hope. A riding accident at an event in Luhmühlen left her legs partially paralyzed. She is almost completely paralyzed from the waist down. She uses a wheelchair, but can walk a little bit with canes and splints. This accident would cause many people to completely give up, but Hanne Brenner was firm. "I will ride again!" For a while, she shared a friend's horse and didn't participate in competitions. Sixteen years ago she entered para-equestrian sport and began to ride again at sanctioned competitions at level E (Training Level). She has had a lot of success at the national and international levels and has been the most successful German handicapped rider for years. In May 2011 she won her first dressage test at the upper levels at a sanctioned competition.

Hannelore Brenner: Through my limitations, I became conscious of the fact that impulsion in riding plays a completely different role. Staying continually on it is simply not possible. Today, I ride with much less use of my body. It took a long time after the accident for me to accept my body and use it commensurate with my ability. It was important for me to realize that every rider has some "construction zone" they have to work on. Some have a kink in the hip, others pull their legs up, or have issues with their balance. Due to the paralysis, my lower legs fly off during the posting trot. Furthermore, I don't have the necessary seat muscles to push a horse together. So I have been shown a way of riding where I collect the horse by sending him to a soft hand. I can't "push" a horse and have noticed that this isn't even necessary! Too much pressure costs relaxation. That was an aha! experience: when something isn't working, you find another way, which is often better. Consequently, I am very happy to be able to participate successfully, even at sanctioned competitions. This shows me that one can score with horses that simply enjoy moving. That is the shared goal of my home trainer, Dorte Christensen, and me. We want to take the horses where they are and develop ourselves with the horse. The horse's essence must always be recognizable and supported. Only then can we achieve the greatest relaxation and the greatest expression. Less is more, even when a horse looks around in the dressage arena. Even then I don't respond with pressure. I give the horse the time, when possible, to look at the problem and quietly ride on. It is important for everyone to make a realistic evaluation of her abilities. I have learned how important it is to adjust myself to my horse so that I can have a secure feeling despite my handicap. That works best with shared trust and the support of a trainer encourages the development of the horse and rider.

(Hannelore Brenner)

Hanne Brenner tells an anecdote that fits well with our theme of effortless riding. As a freshly decorated Gold Medal winner at the Para-Olympics in London, she was asked by a journalist about her riding errors in the test: "How can it be that you actually made errors? I thought a handicapped rider's horse was so trained that he could do everything on his own!" Hanne was speechless. Initially, one could have said that the man was not the brightest candle on the cake. But maybe that would be unfair. He just said (unfortunately) what many non-riders think about riding sports: namely that we trick train the horses. A reader contributed a letter to *Spiegel* (a German news magazine) commenting on dressage in the scope of a discussion of the PISA (Program for International Student Assessment) study—the world's biggest international study looking at the knowledge and skills of 15-year-olds: "The whole to-do about the PISA study reminds me of dressage riding. The horses are taught specific movements, steps, and commands, which they have to perform at competitions."

Based on these two examples, the attitude of the lay public toward riding competition is not particularly good. We should counter the comment about trick training with images and explanations of good riding. On the other hand, we can almost take it as a compliment when we hear from our non-riding friends and relatives "Dressage isn't a sport," or "You are just carried along." But it is too bad, not just for Hanne Brenner but also for all para and regular riders that lay people don't realize the athleticism necessary to ride a horse *at all* and especially to be able to become one with his motion. What if we interpreted such comments by lay people as an indication of how effortless the presentation looked? Shouldn't it be that the interested public could think we actually could drink coffee up there and at the same time read the newspaper? Para riders and regular riders who achieve effortless harmony deserve the highest respect.

Nine Steps to Drinking Coffee

Our motto, which is a little tongue in cheek, inspires us to give step-by-step exercises as examples of how you can prepare the horse so that riding can be as effortless as possible. Since we think handicapped riders have an advantage over us on this subject, we asked Dr. Angelika Trabert to describe for us how she does it. Following are a few examples, which we feel are typically ridden with way more effort than necessary instead of in harmony and lightness.

Angelika told us, for example, that a canter-walk-canter transition is not so simple for her to ride. She has to do it without the support of her legs. It is also not really possible for her to have the horse "sit" and collect in the transition. She must pay close attention so the horse is collected in advance and prepare the horse well for the transition.

She uses her two whips to replace her calves for driving the horse to her hand. Her horse is used to responding with more activity of the hind leg with a soft touch of the whip. "I touch Ariva-Avanti softly with the whip before the transition and drive her that way to the hand more. I try to ride the canter stride with a little more collection and 'sitting' before the transition so that in the moment of halting I only have to sit heavier and think about walk and the mare knows what I want from her. At the beginning I used my voice to help me practice this." Angelika further explains that she initially had to learn to not physically exhaust herself. With her limitations she didn't have the possibility of an especially aggressive riding style anyway, because there never really was a question of a massive use of her body.

Canter-Walk Transitions—Nine Steps to Drinking Coffee	
1	Collect the horse, for example, through changes of tempo at the canter.
2	Increase the weight on the hindquarters, for example by decreasing circle size.
3	Shorten the canter strides, increase the activity, leave the horse alone for a bit, ride the horse out again, ride a quality canter stride that "jumps" well through.
4	For additional preparation, ride shoulder-fore in canter and, if possible, change to travers.
5	Let the horse chew the reins out of the hand and check to see if the horse inverts (goes above the bit); pick the horse up and collect him again (see 1 to 4)
6	Begin the transition: Activate the hind legs, shorten the canter stride, use pulsed driving aids.
7	Keep the poll up, yield with the hand so that the nose stays in front of the vertical.
8	Let yourself down in the saddle with the canter stride staying active and through, relax, and think walk.
9	If successful, praise the horse, and give him a break.

Lateral movements in trot are another good exercise, but it is easy to lose the fluidity. Angelika comments: "Basically, it is all about good preparation. If I don't have my horse actively in front of me and he isn't stretched to the hand, then I can forget lateral movements. Consequently, I work on having the horse truly in front of me. Other riders would say 'in front of the leg,' I say 'in front of the aids.' The aids are given through the seat and the leg, the latter naturally replaced by the whips. But I still have my seat and my weight to take the horse sideways. The mare reacts very well to a shift in weight to the inside seat bone and yields immediately, for example in shoulder-in to the other side. I control this yielding with the outside rein and the outside whip."

Half-pass—Nine Steps to Drinking Coffee	
1	Start by preparing the horse with, for example, voltes, and serpentines to improve positioning and bend.
2	Ride the corners cleanly as a quarter-volte and take that positioning and bend into shoulder-fore. For more trained horses, alternate between shoulder-fore and travers.
3	Consciously straighten the horse on each short side so that you can ride evenly to both hands.
4	Ride trot-walk-trot transitions to increase the collection of the horse.
5	Ride changes of tempo within the gait to make the horse more active so that swing isn't lost in the lateral movement; consciously relax yourself and let him carry you.
6	Begin the half-pass: Prepare positioning and bend, for example, with shoulder-fore or a volte, drive in pulses and let the horse half-pass.
7	If you lose positioning, bend, rhythm, or impulsion, ride a few steps in shoulder-fore to reestablish rhythm, impulsion, positioning and bend, and return to half-pass.
8	Take the coffee cup to your mouth without spilling any.
9	Praise the horse and take a break.

Many riders intuitively feel that they must work harder to improve the trot extensions. As already discussed, Angelika has scarcely any ability to increase the pressure. She has enough to do when riding a bigger trot to just stay balanced and maintain the rhythm. "If I had to extend the trot with more exertion, I would quickly run into rhythm errors. Perhaps the reader can best imagine how it would be if I used the whips in the middle of an extension. Every other horse would probably canter or at least lose the rhythm. Consequently, I have to make my horse more active in advance so that I can just let the movement flow. To accomplish that I touch the mare lightly in the corner before the diagonal, get her attention and collect her with a half-halt. Sometimes I use my voice to help, turn and let myself be carried along in the movement."

These examples show clearly what we can learn from handicapped riders on the subject of using less physical strength. We must merely be sensitive and watch to see if our horses respond to lighter aids. Inspired by handicapped riders, I thought to myself that it must be possible to copy what they do, especially to completely drop the use of one hand at least for a short time. So I built a whole one-handed pirouette into Le Noir's Grand Prix freestyle. This brought before my eyes the fundamental principle that the para-equestrians almost automatically follow: minimal physical effort with maximal effect. Riding a pirouette with two hands is certainly not trivial; but I thought to myself, if a horse like Le Noir can do this exercise and

Drinking coffee in the pirouette—our slogan for effortless riding.

we stay well connected to each other, why not?

Since it worked with Le Noir right off the bat, I internalized once again for all my riding how important good preparation is, and also that an exercise doesn't require an hour of preparation anymore when you are at the end stage of refinement. I have trained Le Noir to wait collected and attentive in front of me for the slightest aid in the test. When I use two hands, I collect the canter strongly, and Le Noir knows that he must now bring all his power together. He shifts his weight to the hindquarters, carries himself and I feel that he is on my aids and in front of the leg. Now I sense the perfect moment to put all four reins in one hand and begin the pirouette. Le Noir doesn't fall apart because he knows that I'm not going to ask for anything else while he executes the movement by himself until I give the aid to ride out of the pirouette. The other hand takes back the pair of reins and I tell Le Noir what we are doing next. Bottom line: Watching the para-equestrians taught us something and we got good points for difficulty with the one-handed riding in our Grand Prix freestyle! But we didn't use the coffee cup....

Damon Jerome NRW ("DJ")—Journal of a Superstar (2)

A Youngster Has Grown Up

Over the last three years from six to nine years old, DJ has undergone a major advance in development. He has gotten more powerful, more athletic, and doesn't seem like a teenager any more. The topline of his neck has developed well and he carries himself in beautiful true self-carriage.

CHALLENGES: Everything always comes easily for DJ. The transition from the M to S level (Third to Fourth Level) was almost play. We feel we did the right thing building a lot of variety into his training and giving him the time to develop physically and mentally so that he can continue to rise to all challenges without worry. I can ride him with a visible lightness. Luckily, DJ has a walk like a "god" and a ground-covering trot and canter. The challenge going forward is to keep the nose in front of the vertical and the throatlatch from getting too narrow as collection increases, and correct him when this carriage is briefly lost.

TRAINING PROGRAM FROM SIX TO NINE YEARS: Rhythm, relaxation, connection, straightness, and impulsion were never an issue for DJ. Consequently, the focus of the program for the collected exercises was to build strength: transitions between working and collected gaits and changes of tempo. We practiced travers, half-pass, and renvers at the trot, adding in shoulder-in. At the canter, we alternated between shoulder-in and travers, also on circles, as preparatory work for the pirouette. With canter flying changes, it was our goal to minimize the aids so they could be ridden with more lightness. DJ is now learning the more difficult movements like pirouettes, two tempis, and half-pass zigzag. We have also added in half-steps. Many observers think we are late starting half-steps at nine years of age. We wanted DJ to have enough time. We waited until he offered them himself.

RESULT: DJ won his first St. George and Intermediare I tests at seven and eight years of age. Unfortunately, DJ didn't show well at the Finale of the Nurnberg Castle Cup in 2013, despite a fantastic season. The suppleness, which won him points previously, wasn't 100 percent there. He obviously didn't feel comfortable in the atmosphere and couldn't show his true potential. That happens. It even happens with a superstar during a fantastic year. Now and then, something goes wrong. You can practice a lot at home, but not everything! Our good boy was very successful at other places with many wins at the S level. He won sixth in the Small Tour at CHIO in Aachen 2013 and won his first international Intermediare I at Perl-Borg.

DJ with Uta

Dandelion at CHIO
in Aachen, 2013

Effortless–
But How?

More Expression
Through Suppleness

Easygoing without Tension

It was a challenge with Damon Jerome NRW not to yield to the temptation to jazz up his already spectacular movement to please the crowd. We have always stuck to our principles of not asking a young horse for 100 percent. This helps the horse be more relaxed in the show arena, which is especially important for the walk.

More expression is what many riders want. It not only looks terrific, it feels good when the horse swings under you and shows spectacular movement. But it is only good for your horse when the expressiveness comes from relaxation, not through tension. Relaxation is a fundamental prerequisite in dressage for advanced training and for the harmonious execution of movements. It is also important for jumpers, even when they aren't specifically judged for it. Martin Plewa, leader of the Westfalian Riding and Driving school in Münster says: "The movement apparatus is exposed to much greater stress. In jumping there is simply more mobility in the horse's body." Suppleness (which comes from relaxation) is the prerequisite for athletic movement over a jump with sufficient bascule. Even trail riding is more pleasant with relaxation, which prevents one-sided strain and tension in the horse. A supple horse is much better able to work out how to use his body. But above all, everything is much easier, looks better, and is twice as much fun with a supple relaxed horse!

It is wonderful to see a trend toward rewarding a relaxed dressage ride with good scores. I have never tried to create more expression through tension. I found it unpleasant to ride that way and, therefore, have never tried. I have concentrated from the beginning on presenting my horses relaxed and with swing and have encouraged my students to do the same thing. When you want to make a "VW into a Porsche" it can cause a lot of physical and emotional problems. I never wanted to do this. I wanted to experience *harmony* with the horse.

In his instruction, Philip Becker puts a lot of emphasis on suppleness as the foundation for bringing out the horse's full motion potential. Uta with Damon Jerome NRW.

Dino

Consolidate Gains, Avoid Tension!

by Friederike Heidenhof

In his third year of training, you can see and feel distinct progress when riding Dino. He can still get heavy in the hand from time to time, but it is a great deal less. I have learned to allow the horse to work independently beneath me. Dino trots off from the beginning with more swing, is more through, and travels with better connection. We still lose relaxation when things are more difficult.

CHALLENGES: It is still relatively difficult for Dino to maintain a powerful and swinging trot without slipping into hover steps. The suspension feels wonderful from up top, but it doesn't come from real activity and swing, which indicates a lack of suppleness (relaxation). It is also hard for us to keep the poll at the highest point and to maintain the appropriate elevation and self-carriage while collected. And sometimes, the croup is still too high in the flying changes.

TRAINING PROGRAM AND TIPS FROM UTA GRÄF: Uta emphasizes collecting Dino more from the beginning to build carrying power. This has worked well and throughness has improved. Uta puts canter work in the warm-up phase early, because Dino feels more comfortable in the canter and loosens up more easily. She lets him chew the reins out of the hand now and then, so the increased self-carriage doesn't overtax him and he can relax. She emphasizes building carrying power and self-carriage by riding transitions and changes of tempo within the gait so the poll is up and the nose in front of the vertical. She also works on improving Dino's step to the bit so that I can leave him alone and get closer to a state of effortlessness. It is very helpful for me to feel this by riding after her. My homework has been to have the horse in front of me with more impulsion, because Dino is sometimes sticky with me. This doesn't happen with Uta and Jassi (Jasmin Simon). So I must continue to work on it if I would like to get closer to effortless riding.

RESULT: We are on the way to confirm the S movements (Fourth Level/Prix St. Georges), but we aren't ready for competition. We will see if we can get closer to that goal next winter. If not, it is still fun every day to work with Dino. It is more important to me to confirm the progress on the principles of lightness and effortless riding.

Dino's trot is becoming more expressive, but isn't completely relaxed.

Achieving expressiveness through relaxation has a lot to do with the power and muscling of the horse. If a horse doesn't have the power to step energetically and to move with swing, tense steps develop, like with Dino. It is easy to confuse this with impulsion or expressiveness based on the feeling, but such steps are absolutely false and receive low scores in a dressage test. Tense movements can come from a rider's seat being too tight. The idea of "hold the front tight and add gas behind" is not the right recipe. It leads to the horse not being able to unfold the potential of his motion with suppleness. If you allow tense steps, you risk increasing the tension in the whole body by allowing this unnatural way of going. It gets more and more difficult to release such tension. It is best to avoid tense steps from the outset and to put special emphasis on suppling work. Training for power to develop more push and carrying ability of the hindquarters will ultimately mean a win for expression!

Summary: A horse travels with a lot of expression if it is achieved through physical and emotional relaxation. For this reason, it is necessary to ride him in true connection and self-carriage without a backward action of the hand. Only when the horse is sensitively on the aids can he fully unfold his natural motion potential and be in harmony with the rider.

Relax, Even When It Is Difficult

Most riders understand that relaxation (which is necessary for suppleness) in the warm up or with young horses is important. But when it comes to more difficult work, they ask, "Do I still have to maintain relaxation, and if yes, how?" The answer to the first part of the question is that yes, it is required in all exercises and movements even at the more difficult levels. Not only that, relaxation is a necessary prerequisite for all achievement. Suppleness is not something that is just looked for during the relaxing posting trot at the beginning of the session, but must be monitored with every single step of training, either to maintain the relaxation or to get it back if the horse has become tense.

And just as important: stay loose yourself! Horses are our mirror. In one of my lessons I kept telling the rider to relax in the half-pass. He focused on strength, and couldn't actually really relax. As I yelled again, "Relax!" he answered, confused, "If you had been practicing half-passes for 10 years and still couldn't do them, you would tense up too!" We have to ask ourselves as riders if we are living, working, and riding under stress that is too high. Can I relax? Have I sunk my teeth into the problem? Am I ready to let go of the riding goals I have set?

If yes, then begin working on physical relaxation. It became clear in the case of my student that it is never too late! In the following year, he was able to improve on the half-pass so much that after 11 years of practice he could finally say, "I can do it!"

When talking about horse and rider we often differentiate between the concepts of positive and negative tension. However, it isn't always clear what the difference actually is. Let's start with the rider. The rider must have a certain amount of tension in the body. Otherwise, in an extreme case she would hang like a wet sack on the horse and be completely ineffective. She should hold the upper body up, head straight, and be able to swing with the horse loose and relaxed in this *positive tension*. It sounds paradoxical, but it is like a gymnast on the high bar. She, too, must stretch herself and build the right body tension while remaining flexible. After a successful performance, athletes frequently say in interviews, "I only won because I was really relaxed and loose today." It is the same with the horse. Ideally, it requires an athletic, positive body tension without cramping up. It is important that this tension does not come from pure power, but that it is developed through athletic training. Positive tension allows a relaxed way of going without exalted, unnatural, hovering, or tense steps.

Just as with the problems discussed earlier, the fundamental rule with tense horses is: Take your time! Don't think in terms of days or weeks, but rather months and years. Horses like Dino that come to us for training and aren't quite relaxed, get our whole program of correct horse care with pasture turnout in a herd, being ridden out, and a stall with a run. They also need to experience our relaxed barn atmosphere.

We consciously delay show expectations and quietly train at home. This is important and keeps your head free! In principle there are not really any exercises in the training program that are different than those for the other horses. We simply put more weight on gymnastics, focusing a short amount of time on a single exercise then allowing the horse to have a break, and chewing the reins out of the hand. Horses get tense easily when they are overtaxed. This can also happen quickly with very talented horses when they try to offer more too early. If the rider makes the mistake of accepting what the horse is offering without the horse having already developed the necessary strength, an eager and motivated horse will attempt to meet the overwhelming expectations of the rider with exalted movements in unnatural elevation. This always leads to the horse stepping too wide behind, weaving due to balance issues, and taking uneven steps.

Naturally, we also make sure that equipment and shoeing are correct and there are no health problems. It does a lot of horses good to have a second session in a day, whether on the longe or at the walk in the hot walker. Most horses develop quickly as physical strength and mental relaxation improve. They can express their natural talents more and more in a truly relaxed way of going.

Practical Exercises for More Suppleness and Expression

The Classical Way

- Avoid making the horse tense by trying to make him move with more energy. Focus instead on his relaxation—also on your own!

- During the warm-up, include exercises that improve suppleness.
  - Stretch forward and downward with the horse staying collected.
  - Keep the nose in front of the vertical, not narrow (behind the vertical) or rolled over (too deep).

- Let the horse chew the reins out of the hands at the trot and canter between exercises and movements, then continue the plan in the same gait (as is required in most dressage tests).

- Ride out in fields, canter in two point, cavalletti work, in-and-out jumps.

- Use a hot walker; work on the longe.

Give This a Try

- Be conscious of your own tension and work on it, for example, with breathing exercises. Give the horse some peace.

- Work on your seat so that you can elastically swing with the horse. Don't clamp down when the back of the horse begins to swing. There is no taboo against seat exercises for advanced riders!

- To avoid hovering steps in the trot, encourage the step of the hind leg:
  - For example, trot-walk-trot exercises.
  - Alternate between working tempo and collected tempo.
  - If the trot begins to hover, immediately ride forward or begin a new exercise.
  - Now and then ride short canters, then return to the trot work.
  - Include shoulder-in or half-pass alternating with straight and forward riding.

- For warm-up: Ride many transitions from canter to trot and from trot to walk and the other way around on curved lines.

- Don't stop the warm up before the horse has really relaxed. Don't ask for any unnatural elevation if it doesn't come through gymnastic work. Take breaks and let the horse chew the reins out of the hand to check whether the horse drops his neck.

- Cavalletti work encourages suppleness and is ideal for training the strength of the hindquarters. This is also accomplished with exercises that require more step of the hind leg (for example, trotting off from the halt).

How Do I Get My Horse in Front of the Leg?

Damon Jerome NRW takes Uta along in the movement perfectly and steps from behind forward to the bit. Uta has the stallion "in front of the leg."

There are certain things that are hard to express in words. Generations of riding instructors search for the right expression to describe something that can only be actually felt while riding, namely, the state of having the horse in front of you. It should be clear that this expression has nothing to do with the location of the bodies of horse and rider. Ideally, it feels as if the rider is sitting a little farther back on the horse, directly on active hindquarters. The rider is always carried along in the movement. Driving aids cause an immediate forward impulsion and the rider is never behind the movement. The horse is active and straight, in balance, through, swinging well, and relaxed in good contact. Similar expressions include: "The horse is on or in front of the leg." Or, "The horse pushes forward to the bit and to both hands." The hardest thing about learning to ride is that you rarely get the chance to feel such an ideal state on a well-trained horse. When you know how it feels to have the horse in front of you, you can get it from less well-trained horses more easily.

It isn't only important in dressage to have the horse in front of you. It is indispensable in jumping. If the horse gets behind the aids on a course, he isn't pulling to the jump and will jump insecurely, if at all. Martin Plewa says: "Many riders have a hard time having the horse in front of them in jumping. But if he isn't, the jump will be worse, and the tempo won't be regular but too fast. That frequently results in resistance, because the rider must correct with the hand too often." It is also more pleasant for pleasure riders when their horse is trained to be in front of the leg, and responding to the aids to go to the hand instead of trying to escape and go sideways to evade the driving aids. When riding out, I feel much more secure when I have my horse in front of me. If my horse leaps about, I don't get so easily behind the movement and can maintain the poll position better. It is easier to keep my horse from bucking or bolting. Having your horse in front of you is fundamen-

You can see in the trot extension how the horse loads the hind end, carries himself and gets free in the shoulder. The movement is beautiful and expressive. Uta with Damon Jerome NRW.

tal for every stage of training and every riding style in order to be closer to effort-less riding. It is also healthier for the horse because he doesn't go for miles on the forehand. So how do I do it?

I can best bring my horse in front of me when I give him the opportunity to take his energy freely forward so that his motion can unfold with swing. Of course, this doesn't mean the horse should rush away. He should remain collected. In one of his seminars, Richard Hinrichs used the term, "Forward and upward!" in this regard. He explained that this should be the motto for working with horses in more advanced training. We have already talked earlier about how many riders tend to hold the poll continually in a position bringing the forehead behind the vertical. This tends to have a backward-oriented braking effect, with the result that the horse can no longer truly be *in front of* the rider. The hind end is blocked and can no longer swing through to the body's center of gravity. Such horses feel pushed, don't work inde-pendently with you anymore, and fall apart as soon as the driving aids are removed. When jumping, you lose the pull to the jump and in the dressage test "the motor dies" as soon as a more demanding exercise is begun. But every horse responds differently. Many horses get hot if they are ridden too narrowly in the throatlatch. In any case, the effortlessness and enjoyment of the ride are quickly diminished.

I always focus on not riding "with the brake on," meaning not affecting the horse in a backward direction, which suppresses the natural forward drive. My horse should ideally travel in good connection and self-carriage with the nose in front of the vertical. I have observed that many riders don't ride sufficiently to the hand. They will ride more frequently against the hand, especially in extensions. This gives the horse a negative message: *If I respond and pull forward I will be slowed up right away.* Ultimately, his motivation to travel happily, and actively forward, decreases. The horse can't take more weight on the hind legs and leans on the hand. In this moment, the rider doesn't have the horse truly in front of her or in front of the leg. To bring my horse in front of me, I need, above all, an engaged, actively stepping hind leg that swings forward. This is necessary for traveling with *schwung*. Activity must always be maintained, regardless of what exercise I am riding. If I lose impul-sion, I can get it back with specific exercises (such as transitions and changes of tempo). I am watchful and react appropriately and encourage the impulsion anew, as soon as there is the slightest indication that impulsion has been lost, and my horse is no longer stepping through forward to the bit and to both hands. I don't tolerate deficient energy—either riding at the walk outside or hard riding. As long as I am sitting on the horse, the horse should be in front of my leg, on my driving aids, and taking me along for the ride. Even with those horses that get hot when they are behind the vertical, it isn't enough to just let the nose go forward. I must attempt to drive him with my leg to the hand so that my horse stays truly in front of my aids for a long period of time.

Practical Exercises to Get the Horse in Front of the Rider

The Classical Way

■ Improve sensitivity to the leg and the move off to the trot with transitions and changes of tempo.

■ Include changes of tempo in your exercise: for example, in shoulder fore, in serpentines, on the circle.

■ Don't overwhelm the horse. Take breaks so that he can regenerate strength. Ideally, let the horse chew the reins out of the hand.

Give This a Try

■ When swing, activity, and reach to the hand are lost during an exercise (e.g. shoulder-in), stop the exercise, ride the horse again with more forward energy on a curved line and continue with the exercise when the horse swings actively from behind again. In no case should you squeeze or clamp.

■ If swing and fluidity of motion are lost with increasing collection, choose a freer tempo again. Consider cantering forward in a light seat.

■ Consciously ride to the hand, especially with increased speed. The horse should softly stretch his neck while keeping the poll relatively high with the forehead in front of the vertical.

■ Seat exercises are also recommended. Develop a seat that is independent of the hand (and doesn't disturb the horse) that enables you to sit and ride the active, impulsive energy to the hand.

Don't Worry about "Inverting"!

There is a stubborn fundamental misunderstanding regarding riding through the poll: Once a horse is "put together" you shouldn't let him fall apart again or invert (go above the bit). This concern is especially expressed to children and young people in lower dressage tests while their jacket is handed to them before the dressage test. The helper on the ground is asked to hold the horse on the bit. He grabs both reins above the withers and holds them short just as the rider would do. Many riders also tend to keep the horse in the same neck carriage through the poll during the entire training session. That is exhausting and tiring even for a well-trained horse.

In young or less trained horses it can lead to pain and muscle spasms and the horse loses the desire to be ridden. If you have truly ridden your horse through the poll, meaning without forcing the poll, if he is straight, balanced, active, and collected, you don't have to worry about the horse falling apart or inverting. You can simply let the horse chew the reins out of the hand so that the horse can stretch without threatening what has been achieved. You can take walk breaks with long reins without having to start all over again. An honestly ridden horse is not collected because he is artificially forced in a frame, but because he is continually trained to develop more strength, weight on the hindquarters, connection, and self-carriage. My horse can accept this self-carriage and connection again immediately when I take up the reins after a walk break, drive my horse to the hand, let him bounce off the bit and get going. Consequently, riding doesn't have to cause trouble. You can quietly relax, take a break, then continue working.

In Le Noir's Grand Prix freestyle, I have put the piaffe in the middle of the walk movements. This shows that Le Noir has no problem going from collected walk to piaffe and back to an extended walk. When I ride these movements there is generally a murmur running through the crowd. That shows me how rare this sequence seems to be.

> "No other movement shows more clearly the relationship
> between rider and horse than piaffe.
> The daily work is evident in the performance."
> — *Richard Hinrichs*

Only through a systematic dressage foundation can you achieve a collected horse that is through, in good connection, and in front of the aids of the rider. Effortless riding only happens when the horse can unfold his natural potential under the rider.

Le Noir

Le Noir—Journal of a Successful Horse (3)

10 and 11 Years Old: Le Noir Ramps Up

As his training continued, Le Noir showed himself to be an example of all the previously described concepts. He gained expression through the development of strength, responded to driving aids to get in front of me, and remained consistently so collected that he didn't invert when I changed elevation into stretching or took breaks.

CHALLENGES: In the previous year, we tested Le Noir with piaffe and noticed that he wasn't quite ready. We didn't try it again for at least another year while we confirmed what we had already achieved. One day I thought we could try it again. And what do you know, the first attempts worked quite easily. And best of all, we could tell that the piaffe was especially fun for him. He didn't lose his suppleness despite the increased difficulty.

TRAINING PROGRAM FOR A 10- AND 11-YEAR-OLD: The passage was even more fun for the stallion. He offered it like no other horse in our barn. I only had to think passage to begin it. Precisely for that reason, we set this exercise aside in the training in order to practice the piaffe. That seemed to be the most logical strategy in order to avoid Le Noir always wanting to passage even when piaffe was asked of him.

TIPS FROM UTA GRÄF: This is an important fundamental principle for all stages of training, not just with Le Noir. Cleverly avoid what the horse happily offers, sometimes taking a little detour.

A

RESULT: Le Noir is now prepared for the Grand Prix and has achieved many wins and placings at this highest level. Together we broke into a higher league and competed at CHIO in Aachen, Wiesbaden, Dortmund, Frankfurt, and other large competitions. Le Noir's strength is the freestyle where I can fully express effortless riding and get points for high levels of difficulty. He has become the darling of the public and receives a lot of applause.

Practical Exercises to Keep the Horse Collected

The Classical Way

■ It is often good to follow a walk break with some trot-walk-trot transitions so that the horse is ridden again from back to front, to let him push off and to increase the collection.

■ Let the horse stretch now and then. When the horse knows this pattern, he won't think all the time about breaks or resting because he just had a short chance to stretch. This is especially advantageous later in the test arena because he doesn't think about a "vacation" with every uberstreichen or in the walk phase.

Give This a Try

■ Trot-walk-trot and canter-walk transitions in short sequences.

■ Canter off out of the rein-back and alternate with walking out of the rein-back.

Effortless–
But How?

Fix a Problem
without Tensing Up

Experiences from Our Daily Training

The eight-year-old gelding Helios is another example, whose development we follow in our "Journal of an Average Horse." Helios is not a problem horse. On the contrary, he was and is plain and uncomplicated. He is more talented than Dino, but isn't a superstar. We want to show with Helios' example how a solid foundation can make an average horse into a really good dressage horse.

Helios—Journal of an "Average Horse" (1)

Characteristics: Honest, Sweet, and Inconspicuous

HISTORY: Helios C was raised by his owner Dr. Jutta Chirita. The dam, about 23, is rather a heavy model that doesn't have the modern look. For this reason she was "refined" by the fashionable and delicate stallion Hibiskus. The breeding goal? An honest, dressage horse for the family's use up to the L level. The result: a healthy, talented, and reliable horse with "country charm" (quote from his owner). From the beginning, it was important to Jutta that he have a good foundation. When her daughter stopped riding, the plan was to sell him. Unfortunately, Jutta got very sick and Helios became an anchor important for her survival over the next several years. No one thought of selling him anymore. The team at Rothenkircherhof wanted to keep Helios, not just because we liked him, but mostly because we very much liked his owner.

CHALLENGES: We had to watch that Helios kept his nose in front of the vertical and didn't roll over. He didn't have a completely honest elevation, so it was our goal to develop good connection and an "A Level dressage neck" at an average elevation. Helios didn't strike you positively as having especially spectacular gaits or negatively about any particular conformation defects. At the beginning, he would wring his tail a lot in the work, but that diminished with time.

TRAINING PROGRAM, FOUR- AND FIVE-YEAR-OLD: Since Helios was healthy and strong, we could train him as normal. His training program included all gaits at a working tempo, frequently chewing the reins out of the hand for improved connection and suppleness, curved lines, and transitions to increase throughness.

RESULT: Helios always gave the rider the feeling that he was strong enough to carry the rider's weight and still stay relaxed. Even as a baby he was obviously very strong, in a positive way. He was one on whose back you could really sit without worrying that you would hurt him with your weight. That is a good prerequisite for further training. His rhythm was steady and calm, but eager, and he was never hot. He was an almost problem-free horse, except for being a little unremarkable. But things would change. His first riding horse tests included scores of 7 or 7.5.

Helios

Narrow or Rolled Over—What to Do?

Helios

At the beginning, Helios tended to creep behind the bit. He wasn't the classical *rollkur* horse, but his throatlatch was frequently too narrow and he was a little too deep. This often happens with horses that are rather loose in the poll. Dino, our not-so-perfect horse, is, on the other hand, rather stiff in the poll and rarely rolled over. On the contrary, he would invert. I personally prefer horses with a soft poll. This is a question of taste because many prefer horses with a rather stiff poll because they are simpler to correct.

Helios is a good example of a horse that appeared basically simple, but who still had challenges to overcome during the course of training, which quickly could have become problems if we hadn't been careful. Horses roll over to avoid a correct contact, as we discussed in the chapter about the basics of contact, "poll up nose in front" (p. 25). It can be hard to decide how to deal with it: take the reins up less to not increase the rolling over, or take up the reins as normal? Many who have to deal with this problem find riding to be difficult and are quickly frustrated. In an extreme case, many riders are at a loss because you can feel really helpless when a horse goes behind the bit. But don't be upset, because problems are normal. It happens to every rider: sometimes you can't progress, but you don't need to hide from it. If you have a horse that rolls over, you can get a grip on it, but you will need patience. Take your time and don't despair!

To try to fix "rolling over" using physical strength, that is, trying to "get the horse up"—is not likely to result in lasting success. Many riders don't realize that rolling over is a problem because it seems better to them than the horse going above the bit. Some horses actually feel quite good from up top although they are too narrow in the throatlatch. For this reason, it is helpful to have feedback from the ground, look in the mirror, or to have videos of you riding. This will help you develop the right feel over time.

What did we do with Helios to improve connection?

The contact will be very unstable at first when you no longer allow the horse to get behind the vertical. But that is no reason to give up. Our goal for Helios was that he should step better to the hand so that the gelding could ultimately travel in improved self-carriage. As a rider, I like more weight in the hand. I let Helios carry his poll slightly higher because that made it easier for him to bring his nose forward. Now I could pick him up in this position and stretch him with a fine connection to his mouth. Through changes of tempo and transitions, he slowly began to step more securely to the bit. This also trained strength enabling him to carry himself better. Taking a lot of breaks and riding for short periods helped to not overwhelm him when he simply didn't have enough carrying and pushing power. Helios learned to trust the hand and hardly creeps behind it at all any more.

At the beginning, Helios would creep behind the hand. Here he is seeking the hand (in the half-pass) and the nose is in front of the vertical.

Our tip: If you have the same problem with your horse, try the following: Lengthen the reins and resist the temptation to physically lift the head up with your hands. Instead, try to take the reins evenly and activate the hindquarters forward to get more stretch to the hand. It can also help to let the horse lift up until he almost inverts. Make sure the horse is comfortable in this position by offering him a sensitive connection. If the horse inverts you shouldn't respond with an immediate take of the hand or you will kill it. I have seen some riders with the same problem that answered every lift up of the head with "flex at the poll." That is exactly wrong and will usually cause the horse to go behind the bit.

Practical Exercises for "Rolling Over"

The Classical Way

- Take up the reins with no slack in them:
  - Move your hands slightly forward and ride to them.
  - Don't pull backward and make sure that the hind leg steps quickly enough and swings forward to avoid hovering steps.
  - If the horse rushes, first slow the tempo, then ride him to the hand.
  - If the horse is lazy, ride forward toward a forward-thinking hand.
- Improve activity and swing, drive in pulses, reduce the aids.
- Trot-walk transitions: send the horse to the hand in the halt.
- Changes of tempo: drive to the hand to increase tempo, reduce tempo without using your hands.
- Don't respond to the horse taking off by forcing the poll.
- Ride leg-yields and shoulder-in with activity.
- Ride curved lines by bringing the inside hand slightly inward and drive to the outside rein.

Give This a Try

- Come to a full stop, then give your hands slightly forward, send the horse impulsively to the hand, offer a sensitive connection.
- Pick him up, make him comfortable there and take the connection into a stretch.
- Give the horse enough time. It takes time to build strength for improved ability to shift the weight to the hindquarters and for self-carriage. Ride in short episodes, sometimes allowing the nose to be too far forward, then take a break.

The Stretch—How Do I Do It?

Riding in a stretching position is an important part of training not just for young horses or dressage horses, but for all horses regardless of discipline. But it isn't simple to do it in a way that helps the horse. There aren't very many horses like Damon Jerome NRW that chewed the reins out of the hand from the beginning—like the textbook says. Sometimes, I have to patiently show the way to the hand and down so that the neck falls from the withers and he stretches trustingly to my hands.

Why is stretching actually so important? Helle Katrine Kleven explains in her book *die Biomechanik der Pferde* ("Biomechanics and Physiotherapy for Horses")

When a horse (Dino) drops his head while grazing, the nuchal ligament pulls on the withers and straightens the vertebral processes.

about the biomechanics of horses that the nuchal ligament pulls and straightens the spinous processes of the withers as soon as the horse drops his head.

This arches the back up. In this position, horses can carry us almost without strength—passively. In order to unload the forehand, muscles need to take over the function of the nuchal ligament more and more so that the horse develops the strength to carry himself. The goal of training is to strengthen the horse's body so that he can carry with the carrying muscles. If the muscles aren't strong enough yet, the horse uses other muscles that aren't built for carrying in order to compensate. This causes the horse to lose suppleness.

The nuchal ligament carries the head passively when relaxed, a little like riding in a stretching position. The horse only has to relax into it.

A giraffe must actively use the muscles to work against a very short nuchal ligament to lower his head. "Relaxing" passively raises his head quickly.

The natural food for the horse is on the ground, while for the giraffe, it is in the trees. Consequently, the two animals are built differently.

Le Noir in the meadow in optimal stretching position, such as what we try to achieve under saddle.

When Dino holds the head high for a long time, for example, by being elevated too early, the nuchal ligament loses its tension. Without the pull on the withers, the vertical processes aren't raised.

To motivate our horses to travel in a stretching position, I let them chew the reins out of the hand now and then and take care that the horse stays collected behind. I slowly lengthen the reins, ride actively to the hand, introduce the increased stretch to the bit, and drive toward it. Ideally, my horse will take the reins out of my hands through the stretch of the neck and the chewing action of the mouth. To take the reins out of the hands means that the horse actively responds when he gets the signal to chew. Many horses deviate from the ideal, in that they invert, roll over, or go against the hand.

How exactly did we proceed with Helios?

As a young horse, it took Helios a long time to stretch to the hand. We had to stay patient in showing him the way to the ground stretching to the hand, and not give up when it took a long time. It is more important to achieve this goal than to work on movements too early. Even if I haven't achieved anything else other than a good chewing of the reins out of the hand in a whole training session, it doesn't matter. It is so important for further training, especially regarding good connection, that I never skip this step. Our patience and training program carefully built on stretching has paid off. Today the connection is much more honest. That is because we gave him as much time as he needed. Here is an example of chewing the reins out of the hand at the posting trot. At first, I let the reins go a little longer and test if Helios' mouth also goes forward. If he gets narrow and rolls over, I carefully show him the way to the ground by riding curved lines and bringing the inside hand slightly to the inside without working backward. At the same time I increase the drive of my inside leg. As soon as Helios carries the bit, I offer him a fine, constant connection to the hand. In this way he stays collected and continues to step actively from behind to the bit. I keep repeating this until he is honestly stretching to a soft hand, with the neck falling from the withers and the nose in front. The nose is ideally already in front of the vertical when I lengthen the rein.

I had to take a completely different path with my previous horse Durbidge. He naturally went in an elevation that wasn't really honest. A good trainer advised me in a lesson: *"Ride him first up to the hand then take the contact to the ground."* I tried it and found that it worked much better. I did it later in the course of training sessions, riding him frequently into a stretching position by often letting him take the reins out of my hands. That led later on to the goal of an honest elevation with good contact and self-carriage. There are many ways to Rome and the right way for one horse can be different than for others.

Helios still isn't stepping ideally to the bit. He is too narrow in the throatlatch and carries his nose behind the vertical

A year later Helios can come into a stretch well. From here Uta can now work on honest elevation.

Damon Jerome NRW ("DJ")—Journal of a Super Talent (3)

A Model at Stretching

In addition to his career as a show horse, Damon Jerome NRW is ideal for riding demonstrations at seminars. We started with several judges' seminars in Warendorf, where international judges studied the practical interpretation of the guidelines using demonstrations and commentary by Christoph Hess of the FN. Practical seminars for members of the FN followed and Damon Jerome NRW always gave a good demonstration. His ability to chew the reins out of the hand in all gaits and immediately adopt a stretching position and stay collected served as a model.

TRAINING PROGRAM: We frequently include chewing of the reins out of the hand in all three gaits in our training program to give DJ a break from elevation and collection and to check over and over his ability to stretch.

RESULT: We enjoy the positive reaction of the audience when we show his perfect stretch then continue to work on the movements. It not only looks effortless, it is effortless for me as the rider!

DJ was always a natural at stretching.

To check that the stretch is correct, I often ask my colleagues to give me feedback because it is sometimes difficult for me to feel it. It can happen that the horse chews the reins out of the hand, creeps behind the vertical and doesn't honestly stretch to the bit. Ideally, the horse's mouth should seek the bit forward and downward. Another problem that can arise is the horse falling apart when chewing the reins out of the hand. This can happen, for example, if the rider stops driving the horse to the bit. When the reins are left long without driving the horse to them, the horse won't stay collected.

All the positive benefits of chewing the reins are lost. If chewing the reins out of the hand is correctly ridden, the activity of the hind end improves as a general rule, and with it, contact and relaxation. The horse goes more over the back to the bit, and the hind leg reaches actively. The horse should stay active behind in the stretch and he shouldn't come onto the forehand.

Our Tip: It can take a quarter of an hour or more within a training session to make a minimal amount of progress with young horses or those with previous poor training. Considering the entire training time frame, stubborn cases can take weeks, months or one or two years. So don't lose patience or the problem will come back at some point to haunt you like a boomerang, causing you a lot of trouble. That doesn't mean that you won't progress in training during this time frame. You can continue normal training and include the stretch now and again in the training session. Don't ride forward and downward just at the beginning in the warm-up, but let him chew the reins out of the hand throughout the session and test to see if your horse seeks the bit and stretches correctly to the hand. It is especially helpful to experience how it feels on a well-trained horse when done correctly.

Practical Exercises for a Better Stretch

The Classical Way

- Ride forward and downward in the warm-up showing the horse the way to the ground. Keep him collected by driving and make sure that the nose stays in front of the vertical and the horse doesn't get narrower or roll over.

- Ride curved lines and changes of direction so that the horse must balance himself.

- Ride the horse with a soft connection to the hand until he lets his neck fall and seeks the bit.

Give This a Try

- Pick up the horse from where he puts himself and take him with you from there out to the stretch position. Goal: Later switch to the stretch position right at the beginning.

- Let the horse chew the reins out of the hand between exercises at the trot or canter, pick him up again, and prepare the next lesson.

- Canter in a light seat with steady connection.

Tight in the Poll: What to Do?

Many riders have trouble riding their horse in correct connection because he is tight in the poll. We are reminded of our Journal horse Dino who was our example of a horse that gets tight in the poll. We discussed him in the chapter on the foundation of connection (see p. 20). Since buying the eight-year-old gelding, Friederike found it difficult for a long time to supple her horse in the poll. Dino was used to getting heavy on the rider's hands, especially in transitions. How do you deal with this without using too much hand?

When the rider answers the horse's heaviness with counter pressure, it is precisely the wrong thing to do. This only sets in motion a negative spiral of strength and torpedoes the goal of effortless riding. Relaxation is a passive, willing process that can't be forced with strength. It does no good. The horse must let go by himself! Horses that are difficult to ride through the poll are usually stiff in the musculature from the upper cervical vertebrae to the withers. With Dino, the energy of motion couldn't come to the bit because he couldn't let go through the poll. He was in the truest sense of the words, "*not through.*" Consequently, he was hard to position and bend and Friederike had trouble regulating rhythm and tempo. This also caused Dino problems in exercises such as the half-pass where he would frequently lose swing and rhythm. When riding out in the fields, Dino's lack of throughness presented a certain risk, because he could be hard to manage in tense situations.

What we did with Dino: We rode Dino patiently from back to front to the hand and caught the energy in a friendly way in front. As soon as he released the slightest bit in the poll, we immediately offered him a light and comfortable connection.

We also longe him regularly and let him walk in the hot walker to relieve tension. Friederike spent several months correcting the stiffness in the poll enough so that Dino didn't go so heavily against the hand. To make riding still more effortless, we ride lots of transitions and watch that we catch the increased weight on the bit with a soft hand so that he connects a positive feeling with it. Friederike's problem was that she frequently rode for too much flexion and ended up putting the brake on by acting backward. The result? Dino was frequently "sticky," which means he reacted minimally to her driving aids. We have worked together to remove the "stickiness" by transforming Friederike's way of riding. A helper can, for example, point a whip toward the hindquarters of the horse. That can be enough to learn how it feels when the horse steps more to the hand. I advised Friederike to take the reins so that she felt the same weight in both reins, regardless of what Dino did with his head. Then she was to drive him to elastic reins while keeping him straight (so that he doesn't evade through a shoulder), catch the increased pressure on the bit with a vibrating hand, and offer Dino a sensitive contact as soon as he yields in the poll and carries himself. Friederike learned how to maintain this constant connection by repeating the process as soon as she lost the effortless feel.

It was sufficient to point the whip toward the hindquarters to free up the "stickiness." Friederike and Dino in a lesson with Uta.

I advised Friederike that she shouldn't demand that he yield at the poll continually, but just briefly check it. This brief poll check can be built in, for example, when you are preparing the horse for a new movement or exercise. Ideally, this only takes a millisecond. It goes like this in slow motion: the horse responds to a lightly driving aid with an increased shove forward. The rider senses an increased weight on the bit briefly, but only until the horse bounces off and the connection is as fine again as previously. Because she doesn't want to ride in constant control anymore, Friederike must be especially sensitive to building an inversion before anyone can actually see it. If she notices that Dino is locking up in the poll again and inverting, I recommend that she return to relaxation and gymnastics, especially posting trot forward and downward, riding on curved lines, and transitions. If a horse tends

Dino steps up well to the bit at the canter and is softer in the poll.

At the beginning of the chewing-the-reins-out-of-the-hand exercise, Dino can relax again and gather strength.

to lock up in the poll, he should be ridden in a stretching position again after a time in elevation. This allows his musculature to relax again and he can gain strength for new periods in increased self-carriage. Apparently, Dino is not yet strong enough to stay in good self-carriage for a longer amount of time, so he tries to go against the hand. Breaks are very important for him so that he can recover strength and relax his muscles.

Sometimes my riding students are unsure how much or how little weight they should feel in the hand. It is hard to say because it is subjective for every rider and differs from horse to horse. Personally, I prefer it when a horse is soft in the connection. Richard Hinrich offers the following helpful thoughts on the theme of "a lot or a little weight":

It doesn't make any sense to specify how much or how little a rider should have in the hand. What is important is to tell the horse how he should carry his head. In a transition there should be a distinctly stronger connection offered rather than a light connection. Horses that have experienced bouncy reins and hands for a long time have experienced jerks on the mouth and therefore feel more comfortable with a firmer connection in

Practical Exercises for Better Throughness

The Classical Way

- Curved lines. For example, reducing the size of circles, simple and double serpentines, voltes, serpentines the width of the arena.
- Include frequent transitions, changes of tempo, lateral movements.
- Improve activity, don't act backward with the hand:
  - Drive back to front to the hand.
  - Collect while vibrating the fingers, offer a light connection.
  - Get help on the ground: point the whip in the direction of the hindquarters.
  - Relax and let yourself go along in the movement.

Give This a Try

- Walk-halt-rein-back-walk in short sequences, always going to the hand and allowing the nose to be forward.
- Ride a circle in travers, alternating with shoulder-in or shoulder-fore, at the trot and the canter.
- Reduce the circle in travers, enlarge the circle in shoulder-fore.
- Take a break and allow the reins to be chewed out of the hand between exercises, then continue.

order to regain trust in the rider's hand. Also, impulsive, ground covering strides require a firmer contact compared to a looser one, so that the horse doesn't lose rhythm and stride length from an undesirable jerk that happens with even the smallest disturbance of balance. Sensitivity in the mouth is individual.

At a seminar at Reken, the expert explained an additional important aspect: "A lot or a little contact isn't so important. What is important is that the horse is in front of the leg!"

The Overeager Horse

For us humans the term "overachiever" carries a negative connotation. Almost everyone has a memory of a student who is pale because he is always cramming, never coming out into the fresh air and constantly doing math problems. Perhaps we can turn the expression around to the positive, because there are also over-achievers in the animal world. For example, the especially active and eager horses, that prefer to go ahead and do what we have only just thought about doing. Le Noir is just such an eager beaver and we are happy about it! Even when he makes training challenging because of his extreme eagerness, it is still fundamentally a more-than-desirable characteristic that we must cleverly guide in a positive di-rection. Just as with eager co-workers, it is especially important to recognize what they do and not frustrate them. This can easily happen if we: a) always give them more work to do or b) drive them harder even though they are already busy or c) if you discourage their eagerness.

During Le Noir's training, his eagerness showed itself in wanting to trot off, or later start piaffing, when I just picked up the reins. He would jump to a fly-ing change when my brain had only thought the "C" of Change, without my legs actually sending an appropriate aid for it. Many riders would be nervous in such a situation and punish their horse (see "c" above)—a sure way to frustrate a horse. Or they ride many more changes just because it is so easy (see "a" or "b" above). Therefore, keep calm and think about the right strategy to get to your goal with the eager horse.

What used to seem like a problem is now one of Le Noir's greatest strengths. When one difficult movement after another comes in the Grand Prix, he makes it unbelievably easy for me today in that he is thinking things through and executes the movement as soon as he has received the aid for it. For example, he might already have it on his radar that the pirouette comes soon and I only have to give *"permission to start."* To achieve this, we must practice together that he really waits for my aids.

Having practiced waiting for the aids is apparent with the flying changes in the test. Uta with Le Noir.

When on a walk outside, taking the reins up without trotting off, helps the horse to understand how to wait. Uta with Le Noir.

This is how we have practiced it with Le Noir: To prevent the stallion from taking off as soon as I pick up the reins at the walk, I have taught him that he can't know what I am going to want to do. During the warm-up phase at the walk, I pick up the reins now and then, shorten the walk a little as if I am going to trot and then let go of the reins. "Huh?" he thought the first couple times, "this is a totally new program. I used to always trot then!" When he gets short at the walk, I take him into a soft shoulder-fore. Then comes the next change in the program: after picking up the reins, I halt, and consciously think about calmness. It was worth having patience and going to all this trouble. Today, I don't have any problems any more even with my walk-piaffe-walk segment in Le Noir's Grand Prix freestyle. Since I have never adjusted the reins before the piaffe, he waits patiently for what is actually coming. This work is also helpful for riding out in the fields. Frequently, the horse wants to take off when he notices the rider has shortened the reins. If you have practiced this work, however, the horse will wait. This increases not just the fun, but also the safety.

Now for the flying changes where Le Noir is also overeager. Many riders have the same challenge with their horses when learning flying changes, especially as soon as they try the tempi changes. What is the clever thing to do when your horse, like Le Noir, tends to anticipate the change? First of all, under no circumstance should you punish the horse, but simply stop calmly and canter off again on the original lead. Don't make a big deal out of it even when it happens often, one time after another. Recognize the spirit in the eagerness, but, of course, don't praise him. Simply go on. For the tempis, it is helpful to ride diagonals now and then without a change. Then ride a canter change through trot or walk. Sometimes, it also helps to stop practicing changes at all for a while until horse and rider are relaxed again.

Very important: Keep your leg on even if you are concerned that your horse will leap into a canter change. He must continue cantering without a change even with your legs gently on until you ask for the change.

As Le Noir started at the S level (Fourth Level/Prix St. Georges), we went to a lot of shows early on so that he could develop more composure. He already knew when the three and four tempis came, and this required a lot of concentration from me in the test. This is the challenge we spent the most time on in our training at the S level. Unfortunately, you can only practice being at a competition at a competition, so that the horse knows that even though canter changes come in the test, he still has to wait for my aids. He learned to wait and today his eagerness to work actively with me is a huge advantage in the Grand Prix.

Practical Exercises to Help the Overachiever Gain More Patience

The Classical Way

■ Vary the order of exercises when you ride:

- Pick up the reins as if you were going to trot off, but halt and relax.
- Leave them long and ride off.

■ Do exercises at unexpected places:

- Flying changes on the long side instead of the diagonal, within a serpentine, on a circle, for example.
- Ride flying canter changes in training a little later than where required in the test (for example, after the designated point).

Give This a Try

■ For anticipated changes:

- Drive the horse on in a counter-canter then consciously demand that he wait.
- Increase and then decrease the stride in counter-canter.
- Ride serpentines across the arena without canter changes.
- Ride a circle in counter-canter without a change.
- At times, ride only simple changes instead of flying changes.

■ For tempi changes:

- Ride out of the tempi sequence into a volte, then return to the tempi-change series.
- After practicing tempi changes, ride only individual canter changes now and then.
- After the three-tempi changes, ride fours, and then a single change again.

The Horse "Drinks Coffee," the Rider Slogs On

Almost nothing is as annoying as riding a lazy horse. Whether in dressage, jumping, or trail riding, it is really unpleasant to have to constantly ask the horse to go forward. Raphaello, one of my previous horses in training, was an example of the leisurely sort. Although his owner Sandra John and I were successful up to Intermediare I, there was no thought of "drinking coffee in the pirouette." It was more like Raphaello "drank the coffee" and we were sweating profusely. We needed a strategy for working with his apathy. As described in the first section of this book under the fundamentals of rhythm and tempo ("active but not rushing"), we emphasized relaxation, throughness, and straightness with Raphaello, so that no spare bit of energy was lost anywhere. This horse showed us how important it is to not squander any energy by letting him fall out over the shoulder, for example. Raphaello confirmed for us that it is too difficult to try to "squeeze forward" a horse that is behind the leg. So, what is the practical way to make a laid-back horse more active?

What we did with Raphaello: We rode him out regularly and used his natural joy of moving to practice extensions without squeezing all the time. We were able to take the improved dynamic back to the arena. *"Stickiness"* in a horse can actually be caused by the rider and confused with *laziness*. Sometimes a horse is "sticky" under one rider, but goes eagerly forward with another. In our daily training we have tried our best to motivate Raphaello and to make the work pleasant for him.

Uta with Raphaello upon receipt of the rider's gold medal—with Joachim Fleisch.

This has more to do with him feeling as much success as possible, rather than the rider concentrating on pure driving. The horse needs a successful experience. Stop the training session when he has worked well for you. We worked Raphaello in short segments, followed by breaks when we felt he had really tried for us. Naturally, the gelding spent the whole day turned out because standing for a long time in a stall can be a major motivation killer.

We noticed that the handsome sorrel gained strength with time. As he did, he became more motivated.

Our Tip: If your horse belongs to the less dynamic of horses, you should first assure that there isn't any sort of health problem. Even a change of season or his coat can cause what seems to be laziness. Additionally, it is good to check out the equipment and shoes to make sure there isn't pressure somewhere. If your horse is simply just "sticky," it makes sense to renew his sensitivity to the aids. Check your own riding and ask yourself if you, as the rider, are squeezing all the time and possibly dulling your horse that way. We have already described what you can do in this case in the discussion of "tight in the poll" and "stickiness" (see p. 72). For example, it helps to ask a helper to point a whip in the direction of the hindquarters, so that the rider gets a good feeling of an active horse without having to drive him excessively. Suppling and gymnastic exercises can improve throughness, until it is possible to get a reaction from your horse with minimal aids. For example, after collected trot or canter, push the gas pedal for a short while to test the horse's forward response and relax immediately as soon as he goes. Riding will get much more effortless. Lateral movements and riding on curved lines (such as serpentines) also help with straightness. Transitions and changes of tempo can improve the move off and can make the horse more active. Riding outside, training with cavalletti and small jumps can also motivate the horse and increase his joy in moving.

I am often asked in seminars: "Should I make my lazy horse more active by using spurs or is it better to ride without spurs so that he doesn't get dull to them too?" The answer always depends on the circumstances. However, in general, when the horse is dull to the aids, it always leads back to a rider problem. For this reason, I mostly recommend that you work on your own "sticky" way of riding. It is most important of all to have control of your own legs. If a horse is already dull and doesn't react any more to the lightest aids, you must find a way as a rider to give him back fun in moving. It can help to energize him through longeing or have another more experienced rider wake him back up again. It can take a while to change your own seat as well as change how you use the spurs and not use them continually any more. In the long run there is no other way.

Making a horse active is less about having the right equipment and more a question of the right use of the driving aids. I can dull my horse with or without spurs. Basically, you should only wear spurs when you have already achieved a relaxed, independent seat and you don't touch the horse with the spurs without meaning to. If you can use the spurs with control and on purpose, it is my experience that it is simpler to make the horse more active with spurs than without.

Frequently changing the tempo was an important cure-all for Raphaello. Increasing the speed for three to four trot or canter strides was sufficient to yield a training effect, after which we returned to a working or collected tempo. It is very important when increasing the speed to always ride to the hand and allow the horse to lengthen his frame. Raphaello's owner and I watched him animate gradually until he could travel independently. We would energize him briefly before increasing the tempo. Then we relaxed and allowed the movement to flow. Don't worry about the horse inverting. If the horse was already collected and on the aids, we could put the hands slightly forward and Raphaello stretched over the top through the poll to the hand and kept the nose in front of the vertical. In this way, we were able to improve his enjoyment and he was honestly in front of us.

Another training horse of the mellow sort on whom I rode my first Grand Prix, was Duvalier. He was a dream horse and we named him our "holy one." Before Duvalier came to us I had no plan to ride the Grand Prix, for this was foreign territory for me. The horse was a fantastic opportunity and I was able to refine the aids still more with the help of my trainer Phillip Becker.

Uta with Duvalier

It is especially important to change up the training as often as possible, rather than rolling out the miles monotonously.

Duvalier's training program included daily turnout, riding outside in the fields, and one training session with the goal of motivating him and sensitizing him to my aids. He accepted the training and worked with much more motivation for me. Within half a year he adjusted to me and this type of training. Riding got easier, which shows that change is still possible, even with older horses.

Practical Exercises for "Mellow" Horses

The Classical Way

- To make him more active: drive in pulses, don't squeeze, relax.
- Straighten through lateral movement, improve throughness with transitions and changes of tempo. Reward every bit of progress with praise and breaks.
- Strengthen motivation and conditioning with regular turnout and social contact.

Give This a Try

- Change up the training: use cavalletti work, trail rides, groundwork.
- Emergency measures: break off the exercise, canter actively in a light seat, then sit again and slow the tempo without backward action of the hands.
- Practice with help from the ground (with or without the longe): ask the horse to go forward and "go along for the ride" with a good feeling.

Bodybuilding for Your Horse

There are issues in training if the horse isn't strong enough yet. In the case of Helios, our second Journal horse, we could see how his motion improved as he developed more strength over the years. As a young horse, he was strongest at the canter. Consequently, we emphasized improving the trot by developing his musculature through systematic training. His way of going gained increasing swing and became more expressive. Now the trot was the gait that we liked the best because he got his feet "out of the sand." No one would have expected that in the beginning. Now we work more on the canter and it is looking like this will be his strongest gait again. Strengthening can change a lot about a horse and affects how we proceed.

Helios

Helios—Journal of an Average Horse (2)
Five and Six Years Old: A Sleeping Talent Awakens

Helios C is now six years old and is almost always even in the contact. He travels mostly with the nose in front of the vertical and trots off willingly on the bit. It has been worth the patience. We continue to have the goal of merely having fun with him. Slowly, a slumbering talent seems to be developing and we are all enjoying him more.

CHALLENGES: Since the canter was the stronger gait from the beginning, we wanted to improve the trot by increasing his strength and also strengthen his weaker left side at the canter.

TRAINING PROGRAM FOR A FIVE- TO SIX-YEAR-OLD: Helios canters more easily to the right, so it made sense to focus on strength training of the left lead canter to enable the hindquarters to better carry the weight. We practiced changes of tempo, and transitions on curved lines to increase collection. With every new canter, the horse must expend energy and it trains his muscles. This does more than just riding for miles in the same gait.

RESULT: When Helios went to the four-year-old test, they didn't exactly throw points at him. We only let him go to one *keuring* as a five-year-old, where he did very well. At six, he was ready to be successful at the A level (First Level) dressage tests, but still better was yet to come.

Canter-trot transitions are not just helpful in the warm-up. They also encourage throughness for further dressage and jumping training. They are irreplaceable at any level of work. Transitions from canter to walk animated Helios to carry more weight behind to prepare him for the collection necessary for higher dressage movements. These transitions are also important for the bigger and shorter canter strides of the jumping course. Trot-walk transitions help get the horse active and collect him. In all transition work, preparation is half the job so that the transition happens without much physical effort.

Here is how we work with Helios. First, we get him active and attentive. Then I drive him into a halt from a walk or trot, receive him at the bit, and offer a fine connection. This helps Helios accept more weight on the hindquarters. Preparation also helps him step powerfully from behind into the new gait and stay in front of the aids. With *up* transitions, we watch that the hind leg responds quickly enough in the move-off so that he moves promptly off the spot.

When we practice transitions and ride forward for short periods, many riding students ask the question: "When the horse is weak, shouldn't you actually ride for longer segments in order to build the horse's musculature?" As is so often the case, the truth lies somewhere in the middle. On one hand, the horse has to be trained and so must be challenged. On the other hand, we don't

Helios's Schwung and carrying power improved through strength training. Uta with Helios.

want to overwhelm him and risk losing his joy in being ridden. It is well known in the athletic training of people and horses that muscles require time for regeneration and avoiding building up too much lactic acid. This makes breaks in strength training unavoidable. A horse also stays mentally fresher when the training changes a lot. Consequently, in most cases riding short segments is advantageous, as long as it doesn't make the horse nervous. With horses that get charged up by a quick series of shorter segments, it can make sense to practice in longer connected units.

Our Journal horses Helios and Dino are very different, but have one thing in common. We also had to start Dino with strength training. Flat, rushing motion without impulsion is frequently a sign that the horse isn't strong enough to carry himself and step powerfully. Helios needed to improve his trot. For Dino, it was the canter where a lack of strength frequently caused a loss of rhythm. In any case, it is important not to increase your own physical effort to compensate for the weakness in the horse. It is still our goal not to constantly regulate rhythm and tempo and not to have to tease out impulsion step by step. This exhausts rider and horse after a while and isn't pretty to watch.

Helios' canter was always good, but it has got better with more "jump" and expression. Uta with Helios.

We ride Dino through many transitions, especially on curved lines. The move off into a swinging trot from the walk or from a halt is similar to dumbbell training in the gym. In response to the driving aids, the horse steps powerfully forward and must move about 1250 pounds of bodyweight with the forward-stepping hind leg. After a series of transitions, we practice something else or take a break. Over the course of time, Dino steps more powerfully at the trot and doesn't need to run off anymore. The canter also has more "jump." Before the canter can get flat again, we prefer to ride a transition to trot. Or, we speed up until the canter is "jumping" through well again then reduce the tempo.

The "jump" in the canter has improved through Dino's strength training. Friederike with Escondido.

Dino trots with more swing now and he hurries less because he has enough strength.

When the Horse Rushes Off

Weakness can also cause a horse to rush. Consequently, we would like to give you a few tips about how you can train rushing horses so they can have more calmness and composure. Many horses go too fast when they are irritated by a rider's aids that are not distinct. If the rider immediately uses the hands backward after she has used driving aids to get the horse to canter (perhaps because she is actually afraid of the increased forward energy) the horse can lose throughness and go too fast. Giving *distinct* aids is especially important. First, give the aid for the canter, ride to the hand, and allow the horse to canter off. With advanced riders at increased collection, ideally, the horse is so collected through preparation at the walk that even the first canter stride is sitting and collected, and the rider can immediately begin to drive with her aids. It helps to think, "First canter stride collected" and "Begin the canter from behind." With horses that tend to draw into themselves, it is generally better to think, "First canter stride big!" It is also very important to drive a *rushing* horse. Many riders want to take the leg completely off this horse because the tempo is already too fast. But, it is better to get the horse to accept the leg, without letting him get too fast. You can do this well by practicing shoulder-in and leg-yielding. You can keep your horse from going too fast in

Practical Exercises for Building Strength in Horses That Rush

The Classical Way

■ Build strength through transitions and changes of tempo:

- Trot-walk transitions, trot-halt-trot.
- Collection-extension-collection.
- With horses that rush because they are hot, longer episodes of training are better.
- If the horse rushes out of weakness, short episodes and breaks are better.

■ Use the driving aids in lateral movements and on curved lines:

- Leg-yield at the walk, in order to make the walk smoother.
- Step over at the trot, alternating with trotting straight.

Give This a Try

■ Cavalletti work in all gaits, also longeing over cavalletti.

■ Ride through the fields, ideally on hills.

■ Water training: ride through water when possible, or use a flooded hot walker.

lateral movements without having to use a lot of hand. This breaks the vicious cycle and enables you to make better use of the driving aids.

To reestablish rhythm and tempo, it can help to gather the horse in lateral movements and on curved lines.

You can't generalize about what tempo is right because it varies for every horse. The tempo that is right for a specific horse is influenced by age, conformation, balance, the quality of the gaits, character of the horse, as well as stage of training. Basically, the horse should not determine the tempo himself. As the rider, I can choose the tempo at which my horse feels most comfortable. I find the right tempo for a rushing horse when I add driving aids. With this as the starting point, I can decide if I want a little more forward energy or take it back a little. A faster tempo only makes sense when the horse is also capable of large movement. Otherwise, he will just go like a sewing machine and lose rhythm. Many riders tend to ride lazy horses a little too fast, which can be fine for a short time but not for long. I have the right tempo for a lazy horse when I have the feeling that he stretches well forward to the hand.

It is important to decide if a horse is rushing because he has too much energy (in which case you should work in longer segments), or if he rushes and gets flat (with no "jump") because he is weak (in which case you should work in shorter segments).

Helios

Helios—Journal of an Average Horse (3)
Seven and Eight Years Old: The Breakthrough!

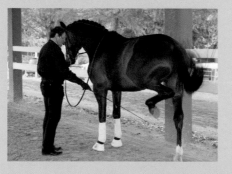

Although his owner never had big plans for Helios ("not every child can become a doctor"), the nondescript brown horse has turned into a sport partner that is fantastic to ride. The previous sympathetic looks from other competitors have turned into questions interested in his breeding. The older Helios gets, the better he scores with his rock-solid disposition and his correct basics. His trot has improved so much that he is now a real looker.

CHALLENGES: The half-pass hasn't been easy for him due to his conformation as he has a rectangular body type. This isn't a special challenge, however, because we have already achieved more than we expected. It's funny how Helios always tells us when he doesn't like something by making a clearly disgusted face. We have never seen anything so distinct with other horses. There is more to come that is unusual.

Richard Hinrichs with Helios.

TRAINING PROGRAM FOR SEVEN AND EIGHT YEARS OLD: To improve the half-pass we work a lot on positioning and bending on curved lines and watch that he doesn't get too narrow in the throatlatch. We took Helios as a demo horse to a seminar in Reken, which was led by Richard Hinrichs, the expert in groundwork. Unplanned but welcome, he declared that using Helios he would show the audience how he uses groundwork to start the piaffe with a horse that has never done it. It was fascinating to watch and we remarked that still more potential slumbered in Helios. Helios responded immediately to the fine aids of the pro. If he had kept going, a few piaffe steps would have clearly developed. But Hinrichs didn't want to overtax the horse, and we took the idea home that there was still more! We began our age-appropriate training for the M/S level (Third and Fourth Level). Helios learned the flying changes well, although he frequently jumped to one side in the beginning. Slowly, we tested tempi changes and built the pirouette preparatory work into the program.

RESULT: At seven, Helios won Level L and M (Second and Third Level) dressage tests. He is strong, healthy, and we believe that one day he can even go Grand Prix. He has already been our "co-worker of the month" several times! This confirmed for us that not every winner is a smiley face from the beginning. Now we wonder if we should call him an "average horse" anymore. Richard Hinrichs' sympathetic commentary made us happy, "The horse beams the good mood of the whole team!"

Helios

How Do I Improve the Bend?

For Helios, improving positioning and bend in the half-pass was a question of gymnastics. Positioning and bend aren't difficult just for Helios and Dino. They are frequently challenges for my riding students' horses as well. In dressage, problems with flexion and bend show up frequently in corners and voltes, in the course of further training in shoulder-in, and later on, in the half-pass. It's also important for jumpers and trail horses to be able to make turns smoothly and in good balance without the horse falling out over the shoulder.

It seems like a paradox that you can't improve flexion and bend without getting the horse straight. If a horse isn't straight, he can't step evenly through the reins to the hands. He will tend to be hollow on one side and fall out the shoulder or swing the hindquarters out.

Uta rides Helios in shoulder-fore down the long side...

...from there she goes into the half-pass on the diagonal.

Leg-yield...

...alternating with half-pass is a good exercise when you have lost flexion and bend.

When I have my horse straight underneath me, I can get flexion at the jaw and bend him around my leg.

To improve lateral movements, we rode Helios and Dino on curved lines frequently changing direction: serpentines, shrinking and enlarging the circle, voltes and carefully through corners. To improve lateral movements, it helps to take the flexion and bend out of the corner or volte into the shoulder-in or travers. Ideally, you shouldn't have to correct the longitudinal bend during the movement. Too much fiddling wastes energy and disturbs the fluidity of the movement and the suppleness of the seat.

When I lose flexion or bend in the course of a lateral movement, I interrupt the exercise, turn onto a curved line, and take the improved flexion and bend back into the lateral movement. In order to improve throughness in the lateral movements, I ride travers alternating with leg-yield and shoulder-in, as appropriate for the amount of training the horse has had. I can improve flexion and bend with shoulder-in but they can sometimes be lost in travers. In order to improve carrying power and swing in the lateral movements I include changes of tempo in lateral movements. Alternating the tempo between more collected and a little freer tempo has numerous benefits. I can check for throughness, test for an immediate response to fine aids, and find the tempo that is particularly comfortable for the horse in lateral movements.

We have come to the place with Helios and Dino where we can maintain even and sufficient flexion and bend for the flow of the half-pass without constantly having to make adjustments. Now lateral movements are typically effortless to ride with both horses because we have not allowed ourselves to "carry" them through the half-pass. Instead, we worked on gymnastics with the horses until it was no longer a problem to perform the movement with lightness. At the beginning, we did a very shallow half-pass and focused on rhythm and connection. Then we rode a steeper half-pass to the easier side, and later also to the other side. Still later, we increased the tempo and bend. If we lost swing, we rode out of the lateral movement onto a curved line to reestablish swing by activating the hindquarters and collecting the horse so that we could better continue the movement.

Practical Exercises for Better Flexion and Bend

The Classical Way

- Develop the foundation and improve straightness through lateral movements: leg-yield, shoulder-fore, shoulder-in, and travers.

- Ride on curved lines: serpentines, shrinking and enlarging circles, voltes, figure eights. Ride corners carefully, especially in counter-canter taking care that the jump of the canter isn't lost.

- For lateral movements, carry the flexion and bend out of the corner or the volte and keep it without having to adjust it.

- Break off the lateral movement as soon as you lose flexion and bend:
  - Ride voltes or serpentines, then start again.
  - Ride shoulder-in or leg-yield, then start over again.

Give This a Try

- Ride around cones or jump standards: voltes, figure eights, or serpentines. Ride squares away from the wall.

- Ride half-pass alternating with leg-yield. Reduce the square as you ride leg-yield; enlarge the square with half-pass. When the horse responds well to the leg, ride with flexion and bend into the half-pass.

- Don't lose flexion and bend as you get to the wall or the half-pass doesn't actually get finished. It's better to end the diagonal with a leg-yield or ride the second track in renvers. The horse must still cross his legs well without bogging down the half-pass.

- Alternate riding the half-pass steeper and shallower.

Oversensitive and Spooky?
The Thing about the Jungle...

Horses that are too spooky aren't really fun. It can rob you of your joy of riding when you have the feeling that a mouse behind the wall only has to sneeze and you will be sitting in the sand. In daily training, this generally isn't the case with Dino, but outside of the arena he can really spook fast. At the beginning, he was very alert at competitions with Friederike and he got accustomed to the atmosphere slowly. Damon Jerome NRW used to be very reactive to applause. As a young horse, he almost dumped me when applause and music started in the winner's circle. You can practice many things at home, but not everything. But we think it is important to try. When the horse's spookiness is defused, the rider can relax and doesn't have to continually try to control him. This is a requirement for the self-carriage we have been talking about that we want to allow the horses to develop. Spookiness often causes anxiety and cramping in the rider and a vicious circle develops. If we strive for a harmonious and effortless feeling when riding, we have to be able to trust our horse. Both the rider and the horse must relax. In our experience, excessive spook-

It helps to get into the psychology of the horse in order to understand and predict his reaction in tenuous situations.

iness can result from how a horse is kept. Changing how the horse is cared for and giving him more opportunity to move around can improve things. Since our horses enjoy sufficient time in the pasture and social contact, we seldom experience excessive spookiness.

We think about how we can expose our horses to as many stimuli as possible. Not just to prepare them for all possible things that could happen, but also to see how they react. Horses react in different ways and as a rider, I must ask myself, Should I hold my horse more or should I let go? Is it better to let him look and calm him, or better to turn away and keep him busy? And in what order? My voice can be calming or make him insecure. Is it perhaps better to be strong so that the horse knows who the boss is? These questions have unique answers for you and your horse. Consequently, it makes a lot of sense to consciously practice specific situations that we know our horse is reactive to. You can find tips for this below and in the chapter on desensitizing in the second half of the book (see p. 102).

Practical Exercises for More Relaxed Horses

The Classical Way

- Provide time in the pasture and social contact. Also more frequent contact with outside stimuli.

- Practice specific situations and approach them cautiously. Don't take down stimuli such as blankets hanging on the wall, but use them for training.

- After the training session, ride out even if the horse has already worked and is mellow. Practice going through water and riding out in the fields.

- Maximize the time the horse gets out in the winter. Use a winter paddock.

- In winter, work in hand, or ride on hard ground outside.

- Adjust the feed: less grain and more hay.

Give This a Try

- Identify your own fears and work on them so that you can give your horse security and clarify who the boss is.

- Fear training: umbrellas, tarps, strollers—everything you can find.

- Noise training: play applause, music, or car noises.

In especially bad situations, it is most important to provide security for the horse. To this point we would like to share with you a short story taken from the book *Pferde sind die besseren Menschen* ("Horses Are the Better People") by Peter Deicke and Petra Herrmann:

Like a jungle guide in the rainforest, the rider has to reassure a horse.

Perhaps we can better understand a horse's fears if we put ourselves in the following situation. You fly over the Amazon River. Pretty flight attendants get you tomato juice or champagne. Suddenly, the first engine quits, and after a while, the second one does, too. The plane falls, there is a deafening noise, and as you come to your senses, you are in the middle of the jungle. All around you are veritable threats to your safety: lurking crocodiles, hungry jaguars, marshes hidden under the leaves all threaten to devour you. Poisonous snakes hang from trees and are hard to differentiate from vines. Tree roots lie like giant snakes. Infected mosquitoes attack you and Indians are hiding around you with poison darts. The emotions you would have in such a situation are the same as what the horse almost always feels.

Suddenly out of the brush comes an authoritative wilderness guide who encourages your trust. Your savior! He is competent, experienced, brave, self-secure, and always master of the situation. He knows the right path and follows it. He protects you from all sides and brings you safely back to civilization.

We have to be a jungle guide so we can make our horse, our children, and anyone dependent on us feel safe. We don't want to debate the right path with our jungle guide when danger lurks all around. Discussions in such a situation are signs of insecurity and incompetence. A jungle or horse guide knows what's what. He determines tempo and direction. We wouldn't think of passing the jungle guide or falling back behind him. It would be clear to us that we are only safe when close to him. Obviously, no one would shove the jungle guide, steal his food, or blather to him. We wouldn't even consider such disrespect that would distract him. Any distraction can mean danger. Horses that trust their human, follow without a rope, without pestering, dawdling, or pulling. They stay close behind the leader and are happy to be able to trust her. This is how I want to understand "dominance."

Tips and Tricks from Experts—Our Treasure Trove

During the research for this book we have talked with many riders and experts and also read a long list of books that touched on related themes. We have run across some interesting tips, exercises, and images that we want to share with you. Consequently, we have included a "Treasure Trove" that you can look through at your leisure. Perhaps a missing piece for you and your horse will be there. Sometimes, your riding can suddenly become more effortless when you stumble by chance over something that especially pertains to you, whether it's a different way of saying something that fits your situation, a picture, or some other meaningful suggestion. So now, here you go. Fully unsorted and loosely organized—everything that we thought was good!

Don't forget to canter travers on circles.

(Fritz Stahlecker)

You get points for just trying!

(Uta Gräf on the subject of "celebrate the small personal successes.")

Ride with the hips through the elbows.

(Phillip Becker on the subject of "riding to the hand" in canter.)

Think of the track as a balance beam.

(Jane Savoie's trick for riding straighter.)

Imagine that you are riding right next to the edge of a cliff instead of the arena wall.

(Jane Savoie's image for controlling the hindquarters to the outside.)

Walk down the centerline in shoulder-in for a
short way to the right and to the left.
(Fritz Stahlecker's tip for improving mobility with less exertion.)

When done correctly,
sitting the trot feels like
riding on an ocean wave.

(Jane Savoie)

The swing (rein-back-
walk-rein-back) tests and
improves throughness.

(Uta Graf's trainer Philip Becker)

Have a positive attitude about fear, imagine it as
your constant companion in all your adventures.

(Jane Savoie)

Canter serpentines down the
centerline with simple or flying
changes, or without changes.

(Fritz Stahlecker)

*The herd in the pasture
during summer at Gut
Rothenkircherhof.*

Le Charmeur Noir, a strong, nervous four-year-old stallion by Lord Loxley, undergoing desensitization training with Stefan Schneider.

Trouble-Free Interaction

The Brave Horse

Danger Is Looming!

Suppleness, expression, allowing some personal space for the horse and letting the horse think things through. Our thoughts about *effortless riding* would be "just garbage" if we were to throw it all overboard as soon as danger loomed. Riders sitting on untrained, spooky, or defensive horses never get around to riding. As long as you don't have a relaxed feeling while riding, without fearing the next crisis, it is difficult to give the horse more freedom and independence. The causes of such crises are inexhaustible. For many riders, this can lead to so much frustration that they think about giving up. Consequently, it is especially important to the theme of *effortless riding* that we devote some time to avoiding crises. We think talking about this will help us come closer to our goal.

Preferably, work on this subject begins with the very young horse. But it is never too late, even in the course of training the horse to ride a volte, to take the time for groundwork and desensitization. When we prepare our horses to stay with us crisis-free, that is "living" horsemanship. We don't have to experience bad situations where we would overreact to the threat, be unfair to the horse, or endanger ourselves. There is not just a little self-interest here: it feels wonderful to sit on a brave and well-educated horse. We save ourselves a lot of trouble from "secondary areas of conflict." We can focus our energy better on what is essential: fine riding in harmony with the horse without exhausting ourselves, or our horse, in the process.

Relaxed riding without crises: Uta and Le Noir in the meadow.

Young Horses: Partners from the Beginning

Horsemanship is an ancient subject, but in conjunction with our theme, it is up to date like never before. For us, effortless or trouble-free riding is based on treating our horses as partners and winning them over to our goals without subjugating them. The author Monika Kramer puts it very simply in her book *Pferde erfolgreich motivieren* ("Successfully Motivate Horses"): "(The thought) that you should want to force the willingness to work is, to put it mildly, just odd!"

> "Wanting to force the willingness to work is, to put it mildly, just odd!"
> — *Monika Krämer*

If we don't want to force the horse, how we think about and handle a horse must fit with what makes sense to him. We orient ourselves to his natural instincts, needs, and reactions. It is an art to raise and train a horse so that his feeling of worth is preserved in the form of independence, courage, and self-confidence. We motivate the horse to join us in rules of the game that assure we work together without crises. We strive to make desired behavior pleasant and undesired behavior unpleasant. Through positive reinforcement, for example, with praise and plenty of breaks, we find that our horses strive later to behave as desired. As a result, doing stuff together is as pleasant and reasonable for us as for the horse. We reject the opposite idea and feel it doesn't lead to success. In our eyes, it is not the right way to punish unwanted behavior thinking the horse will do what we want to avoid pain. Again, Monika Krämer, "The effectiveness of pain is limited. Fear is a poor teacher. Of course fear can cause astonishing feats, but not constant effort! Fear blocks, tenses, and causes uncontrollable reactions." Krämer further explains why the term "make a horse trot" is not the same as "motivation." Most riders confuse "motivate" and "mobilize." The secret to motivation lies in freedom. "Whoever is constantly pressured unlearns how to move freely."

The four-year-old stallion Le Charmeur Noir learns from Le Noir: I can trust my rider!

My husband Stefan starts young horses with leading exercises, groundwork and longeing. He is also an expert on starting horses under saddle. He specialized in this work early on. As a horseman and a veterinarian, he knows the importance of a good and fair foundation. As a dressage rider, I like his work because it makes my riding more effortless. I can better concentrate on the riding questions than if I had to also get the horse started under saddle. Stefan trains his Iberian horses for working equitation. We have learned a lot from each other. It was clear early on that we have the same goals. We want a sensitive riding horse that keeps his poll at the highest point and his nose in front of the vertical. He is always in front of the aids and performs the requested exercise effortlessly, with self-confidence, courage, and fun.

At Equitana in 2013, I had an interesting encounter with Pat Parelli, the American "guru" of natural horsemanship. We were on the same evening program, a big event highlighting demonstrations of human-horse partnership. Pat Parelli and his wife Linda came with a whole entourage of riders, horses, and assistants. They showed the huge audience that horses trained without pressure or force are willing to do all kinds of exercises with poles, barrels, or balls. My participation in this colorful program was to ride Grand Prix exercises on Le Noir in a bitless bridle. A highlight of the show was when two riders chosen by the FN took their classically trained horses and jumped them over tables and benches without batting an eyelash, just like Pat Parelli's show horses that have many years of experience. Christoph Hess of the FN gave a running commentary on our part of the program in his customary bright and competent manner. He made it clear to the audience that horsemanship is not the discovery of the American, but is the central philosophy of classical horse training that provides a century's old foundation for successful sport riding. The exchange about having the same goals was very interesting for everyone, because even the Parellis had never before seen a Grand Prix horse like Le Noir who can be ridden one-handed in the pirouette while bitless.

Two riding styles, the same goal—a harmonious partnership with the horse. Working equitation professional Stefan with Xinoca and Uta with Le Noir.

Natural Horsemanship—An Interview with Pat Parelli

Friederike Heidenhof: Mr. Parelli, what do classical dressage and the Parelli riding style have in common?

Pat Parelli: *The biggest similarity is the long-term view of horse training: the careful, step-by-step training to make the horse into a happy, healthy, and successful partner. The Parelli method is focused on fundamental training of horse and rider, based on an understanding of horse behavior and psychology. Through classical dressage you achieve gymnastic training and the development of fine riding. I am convinced that horses need broad training before they specialize. When I am called to help with a horse that has difficult behavior problems, I usually find that these horses have been specialized in a certain discipline too early. These horses don't have enough trust to be up to their future job. Unfortunately, it is usually the most talented horses that suffer the most. These days we have bred extraordinarily talented horses, but some of them fail in training and are unrideable. These horses don't perform well at competitions. They mess up everything because there has been too much pressure. They completely collapse, mentally and emotionally.*

Heidenhof: What can both sides learn from each other?

Pat Parelli: *Typically, horse training begins with riding, which is the most stressful way for a horse to learn something. That's why we recommend to our students that they begin teaching their horse from the ground and then take that into the saddle with them. It is much easier for the horse to learn something when he can see the trainer. From the ground, we can give him a basic set of aids that can later be developed into the fine work. It is odd to me that most riders don't recognize the value of groundwork when the Spanish Riding School has very effectively trained for hundreds of years under exactly these principles. With*

Pat Parelli training

the Parelli method, we focus on the basics from the ground in order to win the trust of the horse and to avoid fear, defensiveness, misunderstanding, and frustration.

I think our students could learn from classical dressage training. For example, the goal to aspire to the fine art of horsemanship, to experience a harmonious ride, to develop more precision in a leisurely ride out, to internalize training goals that build on each other, to learn the geometry and combinations of movements, and to understand that these movements help the rider concentrate and systematically build the horse through gymnastics.

We think that all good horsemen strive for a trusting partnership with their horse. In the Parelli method, we help students understand how a horse thinks, how he learns and why it is important to build such a foundation.

In nature, the horse is potential prey for predators. He has survived millions of years by running from or fighting with dangerous predators. The horse is naturally afraid of a human because he thinks we are a predator. Consequently, we must do a lot to overcome the potential mistrust. What we consider bad behavior—tension, resistance, fearfulness, spookiness, biting, striking, bucking, rearing, head-shaking, rein lameness, or aggression—are just ways the horse has of showing us that there are problems in his relationship with the rider. When the rider has a problem with his horse, he frequently forgets that it is the relationship that must be changed. If a horse is fearful, he has lost trust, and fights with the rider. Working on the ground with the horse gives the horse a feeling of partnership—a good basis for later riding. For us, this is the most important key for making the horse into a "happy athlete." In every situation, we think about the point of view of the horse and adjust our behavior and the training accordingly. Horses think very differently from humans—what might be important for us is likely to be completely unimportant to the horse. Above all, horses need security, comfort, and play to be happy. If we have convinced the horse that he is safe with us, we can use comfort to teach him our aids.

The important thing comes through the interplay between relaxation and the aids: the horse notices that he is on the right path. We build the training sessions as "games," so that the horse can enjoy what he is doing and doesn't get stressed from "work." Many horses behave as potential prey or like prisoners rather than partners. As potential prey, the horse is afraid that he is in constant danger. As a prisoner, he has learned to obey, but he has lost his soul. If the horse feels like a partner, he enjoys being with the rider just as the rider enjoys being with him. In the arena, we train with objects that help us prepare the horse for a safe ride. Outside, we practice with things that make training in the arena easier. Horses need to come out into nature. They need a natural balance in their life and training. This helps them be at peace and healthy in body and spirit."

Uta with Le Noir at Equitana.

Heidenhof: As you watched Uta Gräf with Le Noir, were you surprised that this was the result of classical dressage training?

Pat Parelli: *We were very pleasantly surprised. This is absolutely the goal of classical training that, unfortunately, is frequently lost at the higher levels due to high performance pressure. From our many years of conversation with Walter Zettl, and more recently, Christoph Hess, we know that a quiet and soft hand and communication through the seat and body language run throughout the individual steps of the Training Pyramid in the classical training system. That is the heart of good dressage riding.*

Christoph Hess recommended Uta Gräf as a partner for the Equitana Show to present the harmonious unity of horse and rider resulting from classical dressage training. We have exactly the same image in mind. At the end, we want all horses and riders to look as one with a smile on the face!"

Our Program for Initial Ground Education and Desensitizing

Step by step out of the trailer: Stefan begins the horse's education with unloading.

The education and desensitization of young horses make later work toward effortless riding easier. As a potential prey and flight animal, he has instincts we can't ignore or hold in check with force and pressure. We must be more clever—and patient. It is irrelevant whether we are working with a young horse or an older one. The goal is always to make dealing with horses safe for both sides, pleasant, and without troublesome wrangling. We have found that this is an enormous help to work under saddle. Our primary motto is: take time, be patient, and resolutely continue training.

Step 1—The First Contact: Let's take as an example, Limbo, a three-year-old gelding that came to us to be started under saddle. Limbo behaved appropriately for his age and was already good to handle. He needed to get used to the new surroundings and the caregivers, first. Stefan and our colleague Anna Schmidt-Pauly began his training when he was unloaded from the trailer upon arrival. The first step that Limbo took in unloading down the trailer ramp was part of the training exercise. It is important to us that horses trust their new leader from the beginning. Stefan does this by making the horse feel secure. So many horses want to jump away from the trailer as fast as possible in their excitement. For this reason, Stefan watched to be sure that Limbo went down the ramp step by step. It's a small, seemingly insignificant detail, but you can learn a lot about the overarching principle.

You absolutely must take your time whenever you are dealing with a horse. Instead of just unloading without thinking about it, Stefan spends time with the new arrival right at the beginning to set the foundation for their future work together. He lets the horse know that he can trust him as his new boss, that he doesn't have to panic, and must not lose his head and jump from the ramp. From the beginning, Stefan has his full attention on the horse and doesn't leave him alone in his initial insecurity.

Step 2—Training to Lead: The initial training to lead begins immediately on the way from the trailer to the stall. In no way does Stefan let him run around out of control, push against the wall, or drag behind him. Remember the story about the jungle. The horse needs security and trust to deal with the confusing jungle of new experiences. This is why Stefan makes it clear with the first steps, "I am the boss and if you trust me, nothing bad happens to you." In the leading training, he has Limbo stop briefly, stand next to him, and proceed on command. He repeats this on the way to the stall a few times, and in this way, the first important rules of the game are discussed. The gelding learns that it is more pleasant to follow these rules of the game because Stefan makes the desired response pleasant. If the horse storms off, he feels the pressure of the halter on the nose as unpleasant. If Limbo slows his tempo, Stefan immediately softens the pressure and makes the horse comfortable. Leading training is done in the first days of arrival. In this way, Stefan shows our new one all the areas of the property and inside the buildings. He continues to build exercises in such as stop, stay standing, go forward, go backward, yield sideways, and walk together with a loose rope. He usually uses a Dually halter (with a rope over the nose), and a lead chain for safety with stallions that hangs loose and is reserved for use in an emergency. It is obvious why he wears strong shoes and gloves. To indicate halt, backward, or sideways, Stefan touches him lightly with a bamboo stick or a whip.

Step 3—Desensitizing: Work from the ground is helpful for young horses before getting started under saddle. It can be done with older horses, as well. We take Limbo to our longeing arena or to the round pen and repeat a few exercises from the leading training. The gelding remembers, "I can trust my new partner." Now Stefan and Anna begin the so-called "sacking-out" process. They fasten a bag or some foil to a stick or whip. The crackling and rustling of a bag is an alarming occurrence for almost all horses, at first. Stefan's goal is for Limbo to overcome his flight reflex in the presence of something scary. Limbo learns to trust his person because he notices that nothing bad happens to him. Stefan takes the bag away from the horse to awaken his curiosity. He doesn't want to toughen up the horse through fear, but wants to win his trust. Limbo follows the bag with his nose and moves it. He notices that the scary object isn't really so bad.

Now for the second phase: touching the side of the horse with the bag. Just like every horse, he moves sideways away from the unpleasant rustle. Now for the decisive "trick": Stefan keeps the bag on the horse's body until Limbo stops moving and stands still of his own accord. If Stefan took the bag away when the horse jumped to the side, he would be rewarding the horse for jumping away by removing the unpleasant thing. But he doesn't want this reaction! So Stefan doesn't take the bag away until Limbo stands still. He has to be quick and follow the moving horse so that the bag stays in contact.

This doesn't make Stefan nervous, even when the reaction is bigger or lasts longer than expected. After a while, Limbo stands still and Stefan lets the bag fall to the ground. He repeats the procedure on the other side of the body because the two halves of the horse's brain aren't connected, so what they learn on one side they can't apply to the other side. Consequently, you can't be frustrated when you have to start from the beginning on the other side. That is also true of riding! The exercise shows that Limbo found the right solution by himself and without force. With a little practice, he will strive to give the desired behavior in the future and won't lose his head and bolt off in dangerous situations.

Anna Schmidt-Pauly shows how sacking-out works: three-year-old Limbo follows the rustling plastic with curiosity. This is the start of overcoming the flight reflex.

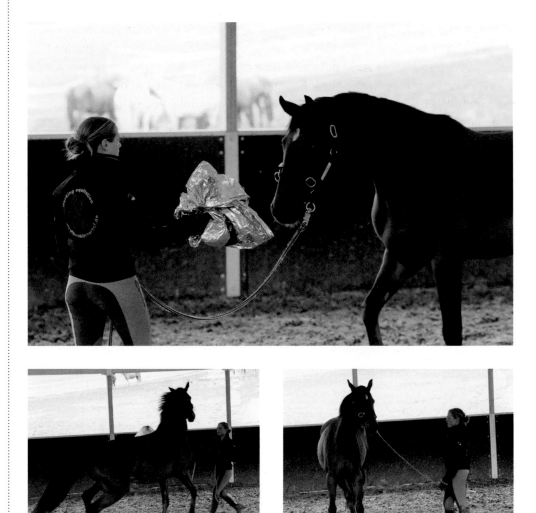

When sacking-out, Anna stays with him as long as necessary until Limbo stays standing.

Anna immediately drops the bag. Limbo has learned that it is more pleasant not to flee.

Step 4—Simulate the Rider: To prepare the green horse for the rider, Stefan continues the sacking-out by rustling the bag over Limbo's back. This is frequently the problem when the horse is being mounted for the first time: he is afraid of an object above his back that he can't really see. It is the same principle as before, same result: at some point Limbo will stop and stand, slurp with the tongue, heave a sigh, and relax, despite having a totally unacceptable situation like a rustling bag on his back.

Step 5—Saddling: Since Limbo now knows the "bag exercise," he is ready for the saddle to be put on, and it isn't a big problem. It is important to be careful when fastening the girth. If you go too quickly and without thinking about it, it can lead to "girthyness" that might not go away. We girth the horse hole by hole, and lead Limbo around several times in between. Time and patience are the magic words here. Finally, we put Limbo on the longe so that he can get used to moving with the saddle. We have already longed him without the saddle. Round pens are best for longeing young horses. In the arena, it helps to have barriers like cavalletti to keep the horse from breaking out. Before Limbo begins the work on the longe, we practice at the halt touching him on the side of his belly with the stirrups hanging down. For the first longeing, we tie up the stirrups. Later, we trot and canter with the stirrups hanging loose so the horse gets used to being touched on the sides.

Step 6—Getting On: Anna stands next to the horse and wants to prepare Limbo for something sitting on his back. First, she jumps up and down next to him. She gets Limbo used to a moving human body, as would be the case in mounting and

Anna demonstrates how she gets the horse used to movement next to him by jumping up and down. At the time of the picture, Limbo already understands. Otherwise an assistant would be holding the horse. Anna Schmidt-Pauly with Limbo.

dismounting. Next, come the remaining steps: lie over the saddle, and lift the leg slowly over the back. Later, Anna intentionally touches him on the croup with her foot. The sooner the horse experiences this, the better. Every rider will hit the back some time. It's a good thing for the horse to not turn into an uncontrollable bullet when it happens.

The amount of time it takes for the steps described here varies, as each horse is different. We take the next step when the previous exercise is confirmed. Anna and Stefan have laid the foundation so that the horse can be trained further without trouble. Even before being mounted for the first time, he learned to trust people, because he understood that being crazy and running around made no sense.

The value of this pre-work to later riding was made clear to me when Damon Jerome NRW came to us as a four-year-old stallion. "DJ" was big, powerful, and had an extraordinary desire to move. If I hadn't had Stefan to work on the ground with him, it most certainly would have been much more difficult for me. I would have been challenged handling him as a young horse at competitions if Stefan hadn't taught him to keep his energy under control. Riding and dressage training were not so bad, as a result. Consequently, I recommend to all riders that they have such training done with their horse, even if he is older.

Desensitization is a solid component of our training program for our horses. Along the same vein, we came upon the idea of playing sounds on the CD. Damon Jerome NRW especially profited from this, because we were able to practice in the riding arena at home with loud applause or other noises coming from our loudspeaker. This is especially effective when a horse doesn't yet know how to handle it.

Anna consciously touches Limbo on the croup to get him used to it.

Initially, DJ was agitated. After the second or third time playing it, he got calmer. In this way, I learned how he reacted without there being hundreds of spectators at an arena watching. I could fully concentrate on my horse and find out how to best handle him in this situation. DJ is visibly more relaxed in real winners' circles and I don't have to worry about life and limb any more, even if they play the Radetzky March. Even Mambo No. 5 at disco loudness doesn't bother him. We chose his nickname "DJ" well!

To prevent trouble in a serious situation, we practice circumstances with our horses that can happen anywhere: umbrellas at the side of the arena, cows on the path through the woods, pedestrians with strollers, crackling foil, fluttering ribbons, tarpaulins on the ground, and even fire. We thought fire training would be something just for Stefan's exhibition with his Iberian horses, but Friederike told us that in the previous year she actually had to ride past two blazing torches into the dressage arena. The advice goes like this: practice what you can practice, so as rider you learn to better understand the reaction of your horse. Despite all the practice, you can't predict everything, and can't avoid every scary situation. Consequently, it is helpful to learn to react calmly and routinely in such situations. My horse learns that I will give him security and he doesn't need to follow his flight reflex. That makes it easier for me to ride with fine aids despite any surprises.

Training with noise: Damon Jerome NRW hears the applause and gives Uta the opportunity to practice dealing effectively with his reaction.

DJ is still a "hot seat" in the winner's circle, but manageable.

Get to know your horse! For active horses like Damon Jerome NRW, training for unusual situations is both something to do and a mental challenge.

To practice, it's best to take what you can find: here we used our photographer's reflection shield. Uta with Damon Jerome NRW and Jasmin Simon.

Even the blue blanket is interesting for DJ at first...

...later, (FAR RIGHT) he relaxes and walks right over it.

Pedestrian with dog, stroller, and pull-toy—Helios stays relaxed. Uta and Melanie Rissel with Julius.

Cows aren't so frightening when you show them to the horse calmly. Uta with Dandelion and Reinhold, the dwarf Zebu.

At four, the stallion Le Charmeur Noir has rock-solid nerves. He even accepted rustling foil on his head the first time. Stefan Schneider.

A natural talent: even Mike, the cow, can't upset the young stallion.

TOP LEFT: *A good exercise when riding out: the experienced horse stays and the young horse walks alone away from him. Le Noir with Uta, Le Charmeur Noir with Anna Schmidt-Pauly.*

TOP RIGHT: *You can even accustom your horse to fire: Stefan Schneider with Marquess at an exhibition.*

For fun, Anna lets the young stallion play with the gymnastic ball even though that isn't on the regular program.

The stallion goes over the tarp after some hesitation and patient requests.

DJ just nipped Jassi while being led, as stallions like to do. Jassi is resolute and gives him a talking to. DJ knows right away....! Jasmin Simon with Damon Jerome NRW.

We make sure our horses have good manners when we work with them on the ground as well as under saddle. It is especially important not to let stallions be dominant. Just being resolute in dealing with them is half the battle, not just in daily handling, but also for effortless riding. Even when it takes extra time the rider doesn't feel she has, it pays off to do it anyway. For example, I insist that my horse remains standing while I get on, doesn't paw in the aisle or in the stall, and doesn't nip me or wipe foam on me. We make it clear to the horse he must keep a respectful distance from us, and not to confuse us with a favorite scratching tree. Experience has taught us that if you let bad behavior go, it will get worse. It is wrong to tolerate seemingly small things that show a lack of respect. We ultimately want a horse that is sensitive to ride and responds promptly to our aids. The goal is easier to achieve when my sports partner doesn't run over me and drag me to the next clump of grass.

Groundwork should never be rough or unfair. That would only teach the horse to fear his person, and that would translate to riding. Timid horses can lose their courage and self-confidence when unfairly treated and become unpredictable. We routinely integrate our groundwork into our daily interaction with the horses. We are always alert to quickly warn the horse about small violations of the rules of the game before it can become a big deal. To the outside observer, it looks as if all the horses are like lambs, but even our horses sometimes test the rules. Often, good manners are destroyed because the rider is not paying attention and is distracted. Multitasking is the culprit. When I try to do three things at the same time, I am working with my horse, I can't react promptly to the small infraction and correct him. It pays to be attentive, focused, and patient. This makes it easier later!

Practical Tips for Training Manners

Leading: Keep the horse active while leading. If necessary, carry a whip in the left hand and point it toward the hindquarters from the side. Hold the rope loosely. Stop with light pressure on the halter, immediately soften when the horse responds. Move backward or sideways with a light touch of the whip, and only use pressure on the halter if the horse goes too fast. As soon as the horse slows down, yield, praise. Maintain eye contact so that the horse concentrates on the leader.

Loading: Lead the horse to the ramp without pulling on the halter or looking at the front of the horse. If the horse stops, let him stand still and look first. Give light pressure on the halter, release as soon as the horse takes a step forward. If the horse goes backward, it often helps to keep him going backward until he doesn't want to any more. Then, go a few more steps backward. In this way, you make it uncomfortable and the horse finds it more comfortable to go forward--his decision. It is important to stay calm, don't scold. Impatience achieves nothing! As soon as he thinks *forward* again, praise, and continue. Repeat this procedure as often as necessary until he goes directly to the trailer. It is better to plan for enough time rather than needing to load quickly because you are under pressure to depart.

Unloading: Back the horse up step by step. If he wants to bolt backward, give a light pressure on the halter until he remains standing, release the pressure as soon as he stands. To practice: go forward a step again before stepping back. Repeat several times.

Turnout: While leading the horse, don't allow him to drop his head to the grass. Always have him stand with his head up then allow him to graze. When you get to the pasture, turn the horse around, and only let him go when the gate is closed and he stands quietly. It helps to feed treats to prevent a sudden bolt. With horses that don't get turned out in the winter, it helps to graze the horse by hand at the beginning of the pasture season. The delicious grass helps him forget to bolt away.

Longeing: Let the horse start moving after he stands quietly in the middle. Don't let him trot until after he has walked long enough, especially in winter, to avoid injury. Also, insist on walking in the summer and don't deviate from this routine. Don't let the horse decide to change the gait of his own accord. If he breaks, send him into a canter again. If he canters on his own, stop him, and wait a while before giving him the command to canter again.

Mounting: Have the horse stand quietly next to the mounting block before getting on. If he starts moving when you put your foot in the stirrup, take your foot out and back him up. After you have mounted, stand a few seconds, and have him move off on the aids.

Putting on and taking off your jacket and horse blanket: This is basically the same as for mounting. It is really very annoying and can also be dangerous when peeling off layers turns into a tussle. It is best to be somewhere where you can take your time to calmly teach the horse without bothering someone else. Young horses need to be accustomed to jackets and blankets from the ground first. Have the assistance of a helper for putting blankets on and taking them off.

Stefan Schneider with Damon Jerome NRW at work with the long lines

Trouble-Free Interaction

"Easygoing" with Groundwork and Trail Course

Longeing Helps Correct Issues

We talked earlier about our Journal horse Dino originally having problems with *throughness*. He got heavy on the hand, especially in transitions. Consequently, we worked him regularly on the longe. He first learned to respond to voice commands to trot, canter, and halt. This was helpful because we could practice transitions on the longe. When Dino leaned on the bit in transitions on the longe, Friederike could stay relaxed because her horse had to learn to "bump" off the bit himself as a result of her driving aids. We worked at first on trot-walk transitions, then canter-trot transitions, and changes of tempo within a gait. Dino responded well to the program. Longeing supported the rest of the training perfectly.

When I logically build longeing into a training program, I can save myself a lot of trouble riding when I have a lot of horses. Longeing work is more than just making the horse move from the ground. Longeing can further a whole list of training goals, and also be the solution to problems. For those not already experienced in longeing, it is good to take a longeing course or ask an experienced trainer how best to proceed. There are also good books that describe how to rig the equipment, safety issues you need to watch for, and where you should longe. The subject is limitless, but we will restrict it to how we build longeing into the training of our horses.

How often we longe varies, usually one to two times a week. Some horses, more often, for example, youngsters, and some, less often. We use a longe line, longeing surcingle, and a Vienna rein or side-reins. It is important to use side-reins because the horse needs to learn through longeing to respond to the driving aids and "bump" off the bit. Longeing without side-reins only serves traveling forward, and has little value for gymnastic training. Normally, we build longeing into the training as an alternative to riding because we don't want to train every horse every day under saddle. This provides some variety but also intentional gymnastic, strength, and conditioning training. We can develop activity, throughness, and looseness. Work on the longe has still more advantages: we can train the horse while excluding a lot of disturbances, namely ourselves riding. Sometimes, problems develop during riding as a result of a bad rider-horse chain reaction. For example, when the horse is "sticky," the rider drives more. The horse gets more "stuck" because the driving aids don't come through. In this case, it can help to stop riding and reestablish joy in going and swing in the horse. The horse that is schooled on the longe responds better to the voice and the longe whip than to the driving leg of the rider.

Longeing can save a rider a lot of trouble. Friederike with Dino.

The skillful longeing trainer can adjust the command to trot to match the exact moment when the inside hind leg steps forward. The hind leg is effectively activated because the horse is free of the rider's weight, and likewise free of a possible braking backward hand action or a less-than-supple seat. An additional advantage to longeing work as compared to riding is the speed of reaction. Most riders are too slow in softening in response to the desired push off the bit. On the longe, the horse is immediately rewarded with a more comfortable feeling in his mouth.

Or, take the example of a horse that is tight in the back, which makes it hard for the rider to sit, and consequently the horse more uncomfortable. The horse gets even tighter in the back. Longeing can help with this situation as well, because you take the rider out of the problem and the horse can be brought "to the spur" in another way. Longeing is, therefore, a big help. Since I have learned how to do it correctly, it is a solid training alternative. We encourage looseness on the longe with a relaxed walk, trot, and canter. The equipment should be fastened on the horse so that he does not come behind the vertical. Cavalletti work can also help strengthen and develop swing in the back, give the horse variety, and help horses that are too fast find a quieter tempo.

Practical Longeing Exercises for Effortless Riding

Suppleness: Transitions, changes of tempo and cavalletti work encourage suppleness. The back can swing better without the rider's weight. Longeing can provide stress-free exercise and mental relief from training under saddle.

Flexing and Bending: Adjust the horse to the curve of the circle with a slight shortening of the inside side-rein. Try this: feed the longe line through the bit and fasten it to the surcingle. You can ask for more flexing then soften. Change direction frequently.

Tempo is too fast: Longeing over cavalletti slows the tempo and can create more swing and ground-covering motion.

Lacking forward energy: Energize the horse through transitions and changes of tempo and train the horse to trot off. The forward desire is often greater without the rider's weight.

Stretching position: Drive the horse to the bit with longer side-reins. The horse will look for the way down himself.

Contact issues and throughness: Yield in the poll during transitions, bouncing off the bit without the hand effect of the rider.

Tension: Use the longe to reduce overeagerness to move. Tension is released by freedom of movement without the rider's weight, a chance to buck, and by letting the horse get accustomed to outside stimuli without a potentially frightened rider.

Work with Long Lines

Damon Jerome NRW proved himself to be a born candidate for work on long lines. As a four-year-old stallion, he was full of uncontrollable energy and the need to move. We had to think a lot about how to keep him busy, and, at the same time, progress in his training to be a riding horse. We took a lot of trouble to make dealing with him and riding him easy for later. Stefan made it a lot of fun working with the horse from the ground, and I benefited from it!

Working with long lines has to be learned, but it is worth talking about it a little. Until I got to know Stefan, I never would have thought it could do so much for riding as well as just the relationship with the horse. Groundwork welds horse and rider together in a way that gives them a totally different partner relationship. It is an ideal measurement of the degree of understanding I have for my horse. When I walk behind him with the long lines, he has to trust me, and I have to trust him. I was astounded, at first, with all that Stefan can do: he has the horse do all kinds of figures in the arena, steers him through the woods along narrow paths, and trains him up and down hills in the fields. He practices working in water in the creek, drives him over cavalletti, or lets him figure out obstacles on the trail course.

I am sure that work on long lines helped Damon Jerome NRW to better understand who the boss is in the ring. It was obviously significant that Stefan was responsible for the groundwork, and I for the rest of the training as rider. It takes a lot of experience to steer such an agile package of power from the ground and you have to be in good condition to keep up with a giant stride. Stefan is quick and agile. He forgets everything around him when working with long lines and concentrates fully and completely on the horse. Scarcely any movement by the horse escapes him without his appropriate reaction. This fine steering is the result of many years of practice. It is invaluable to begin with a good, calm horse that takes directions. Here is how Stefan proceeds:

Voice Commands: Stefan uses a manageable set of voice aids: a calming "Ho," an encouraging click or kissing noise as a forward aid, "Good job," or "Good boy," as praise. I also use the kissing sound to support the driving aids.

Praise with the voice helps my horses relax.

Work on long lines has to be learned, but can be of great help for effortless riding. Stefan with Damon Jerome NRW.

Respect: Damon Jerome NRW has learned to better respect the rider and the ground personnel through work with long lines. It's easier, as a general rule, to teach manners—for example, to stand still while mounting. I don't have to deal with being "buffaloed" and can start with training right away.

Forward: Work on long lines has only one direction to begin with: forward, that is *away* from the human, regardless of what happens. This helps hugely with riding. I can much more easily correct dangerous situations or errors in training when moving forward when the horse already has this idea like a reflex in his head.

Yielding: Long lines can also teach the horse to move sideways and backward as well as forward. It helps me practice lateral movements when he has already learned to yield to a sideways driving aid from the ground.

Confidence: DJ is not exactly lacking in this, but there are horses that blossom right away. They have to rely on themselves more in long lines work than when they have a rider sitting on them. The horse has to go ahead of the rider, thus, gaining courage and self-confidence. It is a huge win for dressage work when a timid horse learns to trust himself more.

Desensitization: Fearful horses benefit a great deal from being shown around while on long lines. Stefan takes them to see our cows that we keep for working equitation training, or past umbrellas, tarps, and other obstacles. The benefit for later riding is obvious.

As a serious dressage rider with my competition horse Kringel, it was hardly conceivable a few years ago to ride around cones. In the past, we didn't think out of the box enough to see what riders of other disciplines were doing to achieve similar goals. They often use different and, sometimes, more creative exercises. I have come to know these exercises through my husband who trains his horses for trail competition.

I have experienced how the rideability of his horses improved and what a positive influence this was on the whole training as well as his relationship with the

Opening and closing gates is good exercise for coordination with the horse. Stefan with Xinoca.

Riding backward through the pole L increases throughness.

Dandelion see ghosts. So Uta practices with him now and then in Stefan's working-equitation arena.

horses. Working equitation stems from the tradition of the working horse and is therefore based on effortlessness. For example, when Stefan wants to close a cattle gate from horseback, his horse must react to very fine aids.

In my eyes, trail riding is not contradictory to classical dressage training because it is also based on the foundation of the Training Scale. By this I mean that trail exercises are not a circus act, but are an enriching change from dressage training. If dressage work follows too narrow a pattern, the horse can get mentally dull.

Consequently, I think it is a good idea to break out of the routine and to have creative alternatives. As dressage riders, we use only straight lines, voltes, circles, and serpentines. By using poles and cones, we can increase the possibilities of multiple lines to follow and exercises to undertake. A four-leaf clover made of four cones can be ridden around and is nothing more than a series of half-voltes. But it provides a line to follow that can be challenging to ride and can only be correctly ridden if the horse is "through." The goal is the same: to ride figures or exercises that are fun for horse, rider and spectators as a harmonious unit on a through horse. A positive side effect is that the horse gets accustomed to additional external stimuli, which helps to make riding more secure. A horse that has been exposed to barrels, cones, fluttering banners, bridges, or tarps at home is very likely going to be more relaxed later at a competition or out in the countryside.

I have tried Stefan's trail course with Le Noir and also with Dandelion. The horses enjoyed seeing and doing something different. I was able to see if this was especially challenging for them. Stefan's Lusitanos are somewhat smaller and therefore easier to turn, but my two horses could canter around the cones in serpentines with flying changes in the middle just like their Portuguese friends. Finally, we went under flutter bands hanging down, over a bridge and by our wooden cow. I could ring the bell and open the gate. We think that such a program is a great addition to effortless riding, as every rider can be creative with it.

The horses are exposed to more and weaknesses in throughness can be positively influenced. So, it pays to think out of the box!

Ideas for a Trail Course

Cones: Place three to four cones in a line. The distance between the cones depends on the size and the level of training of the horse. Ride through in a serpentine at first at the walk, then at the trot, and later at the canter. Take note of correct flexing and bend. Maintain activity and tempo.

Barrels: Take two rain barrels and place them about 4 to 6 feet apart and ride figure eights around them. For more advanced horses, ride pirouettes around the barrels.

Poles: Place two poles parallel to each other on the ground. Ride forward and backward between the poles. To increase the difficulty, make an L out of the poles and back up through it.

Sideways: Place one pole on the ground. With the horse's forehand on one side of the pole and the hind end on the other side of the pole (the pole is under the middle of the horse), move the horse sideways along the pole.

Gates: A good exercise for developing fine communication between horse and rider is to open and close a gate from horseback. Move sideways to the closed gate, open it, hang on to it and have the horse move forward step by step. Turn the horse and close the gate.

Bridge: There are a lot of advantages to acquainting a horse to walking over unfamiliar ground. You need a stable wood platform without sharp edges. This is good training for walking onto the loading ramp of a trailer.

Be creative: Look around your barn for places that are unfamiliar to the horse and think about an exercise. For example, while riding, take your jacket off and place it on a vertical standard and pick it up again; put up flutter banners and ride through them, etc.

We think that such exercises can be helpful in bringing a little variety to everyday training for advanced dressage horses or jumpers. The new stimuli appeal to their desire to play. Earlier, you learned from horse psychologist Wilhelm Blendinger that the concepts of "work" and "sport" are foreign to the horse. You can use the drive to play to stimulate and motivate so the horse has fun working with you. In our eyes, this is a central prerequisite for fine, effortless riding.

Dandelion has helped us understand that it is logical to be familiar with the horse's psyche if you want him to be your partner for a long time and help him achieve his goals, too.

Dandelion—Journal of a Newcomer (1)
Eight Years Old and Hot to Trot!

HISTORY: Our bay gelding by de Niro is a good example of how patient training for more relaxation pays off later. When Dandelion came to our barn as an eight-year-old, we all agreed that he was a good one! Previously, he had been ridden by a very successful and experienced trainer and brought a long way-- his pirouettes were already quite good and he was familiar with piaffe. When the owner's daughter gave up riding, Dandelion was for sale.

CHALLENGES: From the beginning, Dandelion moved with a lot of power, elasticity, and forward energy. It would take a while to get him more relaxed at competitions. At the beginning, he was very hot with the tempi changes. He needed most of all to become more laid back.

TRAINING PROGRAM AS AN EIGHT- AND NINE-YEAR-OLD: It did him a lot of good to be able to live in a herd with other horses. Although Dandelion is very dynamic, he is actually a rather timid type that benefits from a lot of social contact. We have also tried to acquaint him with as much outside stimuli as possible because he tends to stare at something unexpected in the arena. If he gets hot in training, I calm him with my voice, recover the tempo on curved lines and in lateral movements so that I can still give with the hand and ride him to it. I have patiently repeated this until he has become quieter in rhythm and tempo.

TIPS: When working with a dynamic horse like Dandelion, it is important not to get nervous yourself. Dynamism is his strength, because a high degree of willingness to perform is hiding in there. In training, I try to transform what I could consider as a weakness into strength, without taking away his courage and self-confidence. I will need to double these characteristics later in the arena!

RESULT: We showed Dandelion at eight years old in class M (Third Level), at nine he was successful at the S level (Fourth Level/Prix St. Georges) and achieved 15 wins! He gained more competition experience and we could continue to work on more calmness.

Dandelion

Uta with Dandelion in training.

Out in the winter paddock at Gut Rothenkircherhof.

Trouble-Free Interaction

A Question of Horse Care

Outside in Wind and Weather

As we were writing this book, the first snow was falling and the temperature sank well below the freezing point. Some already know that we train without a normal indoor arena and ride only in emergency situations under the tarp roof of our run-in shed. Since we only have 18 meters on the long side and three columns in the middle, we ride outside if at all possible, even with wind and weather. We know this is unusual for competition riders. In our view, keeping and training horses in the fresh air has a positive side. Many riders put their horses regularly in the pasture and enjoy leaving the four walls of the indoor arena, with one limitation: most stay inside when it is frosty, rainy, or stormy. Riders who have an indoor arena available don't ride under unpleasant conditions outside when it is temptingly quiet, dry, and warm inside. We would honestly do the same thing. Because we know this, we have decided against an indoor arena so as not to lose the many advantages of fresh-air training. We enjoy being outside all year long and see this as an advantage for our

Uta with Dandelion at the Grand Prix in Wiesbaden— in pouring rain.

effortless riding. Our horses are very relaxed when training and are comfortable with everything that nature and the environment have to offer. Rain, wind, and cold—we encounter that regularly at competitions. We can stay relaxed ourselves and not be horrified when everything is flying around or when the dressage arena looks like a lake.

That's how it was, for example, at the Grand Prix in Wiesbaden in 2013. It rained so hard that we not only were completely soaked from above but also had to ride in water. But we were used to it. It is often possible to train outside with frost or snow because we have footing made of textile pieces that don't freeze as quickly.

Like a snowball: Uta with Dandelion training in the winter.

There isn't bad weather at Rothenkircherhof, only lots of clothes...!

But wasn't our subject *effortless riding*? Isn't it actually more trouble to get wet when riding, to freeze, and to hang onto your hat in stormy weather? This is how others feel and perhaps not everyone can like or understand our way. But I notice when I am teaching that horses are very feisty in the winter, and that can cause trouble when riding. It is difficult to work with a horse in a reasonable way when he is constantly about to explode. Often multiple horses are in a similar mood. There only needs to be a small incident for a collective explosion. Some riders can stay calm. Others try to get their horse in hand with too much control. It is difficult to use all the ideas and recommendations we have written about concerning effortless riding, because under such circumstances it is all about survival for weeks during the winter. So here are some tips to get out of the winter indoor arena routine.

To warm up, Uta rides Le Noir in the winter across the frozen pasture.

Ideas for Effortless Winter Training

Stay outside: Don't let summer end! Take a walk around outside in all weathers before or after training in the indoor. If you stay inside for a few weeks due to bad weather, you risk the horse becoming spooky. The horse stays relaxed if you stay with it.

Footing: Have your barn help harrow the outside arena before the frost. You can then use it for walking because the footing doesn't freeze lumpy.

Ride out: You can ride outside even when it is windy, muddy, or cold. Dress warmly and it is almost always okay to walk outside. When the footing allows it, trot and canter, as well. Be careful with frozen or very deep footing. It is best to ride very feisty horses outside after training.

Second session: If you have enough time, do your horse a favor and have a second session in a day—especially if he can't go out to the pasture. Change up which horse gets another ride in the day. Alternatives: hot walker, longeing, walking under saddle. If you yourself don't have time, it is worth the money to pay someone.

Pasture or paddock: Don't take a break, but put the horses out in bad weather, if at all possible. Better to go out regularly for a short time than not at all!

Summer at Rothenkircherhof.

Diamond's Peppi takes a shower.

Uta with Dandelion in summer training.

The herd enoys the late summer.

The Norwegian Kiony lets the sun shine on his coat....

Damon Jerome NRW in pouring rain: it doesn't seem to bother him since he has a choice. His paddock door is open...

Happy being lazy in the snow.

The old cloister Rothenkircherhof in winter.

Playing to pass the time in winter.

Social contact with others of their own kind makes horses calm.

Damon Jerome NRW—clipped for the Frankfurt Festival competition—enjoys the snow.

It is fun to ride in the snow when horse and rider are relaxed. Friederike on Dino in a lesson with Uta.

Turnout and Social Contact

According to Wilhelm Blendinger, the horse's psychology we have already discussed, the most frequent cause of neurotic behavior is insufficient opportunity to satisfy the need to move. If we can avoid this, we have stopped an important source of trouble. We are lucky to have large pastures and a winter paddock available. We know that not every rider can let his horse outside in the winter, but we think that keeping horses in the winter in this way can spare us a lot of trouble when riding. Our horses are moving all day, they don't freeze, and they have the opportunity to play with other horses. This makes them mentally calmer and prepares them physically for training. I don't worry about cold, stiff joints and tendons. I notice that in the walk phase and when I start to trot the horses are already supple.

Many riders worry about the risk of injury with frozen ground in the paddocks and pastures. We have observed that our horses travel over the holes and lumps of the frozen ground skillfully, because they have learned to take care of themselves. They have turnout without interruption so they don't have a reason to run around bucking. If you wait until the sun is shining after the wet autumn, it is usually too late. The ground is hard, the air is cold, and the horses aren't used to it. The desire to move has already been bottled up and will be released. After a few days or weeks of no social contact, playful wrangling with buddies outside is a welcome change. That presents risk of injury. But, whoever stays with it and turns out her horses in any weather will enjoy relaxed riding, outside as well as in the arena, and will be able to fully concentrate on the program for less strenuous riding. There isn't a guarantee of no accidents out in the pasture, our owners know that, but there is none in the stall or for training either.

There are a lot of advantages to putting horses outside in the winter for effortless riding.

A Small Anecdote in Passing

by Friederike Heidenhof

As we were shooting the title photo for our new DVD, it was so hot that we came up with the idea of a sun umbrella. Originally, we had planned to let Le Noir sniff the umbrella. The stallion was disinterested and the pictures were boring. Then we thought of approaching the horse with the open umbrella and happily awaited his excited look. It didn't happen and we got rid of these pictures, too. So then Uta got the idea of taking the umbrella along while in the saddle. The photographer and assistants standing around wondered about it and Le Noir probably had his own thoughts. Nevertheless, he didn't react to that either, and only once pricked his ears for the photo. As a final resort, we got the flag that is used to "sack out" the young horses. Finally, Le Noir pricked his ears and we got a couple of pretty photographs. It would have been more entertaining than the umbrella photo to capture the bit players jumping around and making noise until we had the picture in the can. For active situations, the horses at Rothenkircherhof are just too relaxed....

Uta with Le Noir

The Cool Rider

Effortless Riding Starts in Your Head!

The "Psycho" Rider

In the first chapter, The "Psycho Horse," we learned from Wilhelm Blendinger that we should meet the horse in his desire to play as much as possible. Since work is fundamentally foreign to horses, his desire to play is the key to lightness. But what if we as riders stand in the way? When we lose effortlessness in riding, it can be that we are a part of the problem, namely that we are blocked mentally. Many know the unpleasant feeling when something in the relationship between horse and rider is in a bad way. It could be that you haven't found a real emotional connection to the horse or you are stuck in a riding issue. Your favorite hobby can become a burden. When you are tense and stressed, you will think perhaps, "Another burden in an already problem-loaded day—no one needs that."

> "I don't know whether riding dressage makes people crazy,
> or if only crazy people ride dressage."
> — *Richard Hinrichs*

This can be frustrating to figure out. Which comes first: chicken or egg? Am I unhappy as a rider, because riding is hard for me? Or is riding hard for me because I am tense and stiff for some reason? Effortless riding is not just a question of technique, but to a high degree it is a question of attitude. In competitive sport we work with mental training to get closer to personal goals. Such mental training also makes good sense for amateurs or trail riders.

Effortless riding depends on how you look at it. If you, by nature, think it is appropriate or worthwhile

Horses live in the here and now and enjoy the moment. They don't have trouble until we riders try to do something to them.

to constantly kill yourself, why should it be any other way when riding? Even if it weren't enough that you feel uncomfortable, it is reasonable to try to change for your horse's sake, because an arduous struggle in the saddle causes a lot of trouble for the horse. In all other areas of life we regard effort and trouble to be normal because it only affects us. In riding, however, it also affects our horse!

In the best scenario, riding can be considered a type of therapy for yourself. Dealing with horses can help you find out a lot about yourself. "The horse is a mirror of yourself. Whoever is angry with his horse should likewise be angry at himself," says Rudolf G. Binding. I project to my horse what I as a human being am currently living through. So, in riding, I harvest the problems I have previously put in the horse. When I am tight and tense, it is likely that the horse is also stiff and can't relax. Chicken or egg? Sometimes, we don't know for sure but it is worth thinking about in any case.

Riding and interacting with horses offers us an enormous opportunity to learn about ourselves and to make positive changes. To achieve effortlessness isn't so much about teaching the horse something, rather it is about the horse teaching us something about riding. Riding is more than just a sport. Compared to a fitness club, riding is fascinating, because we deal with an animal as a partner and can learn with him our whole life—and progress. If all goes well, we can ride into old age. There is no reason to believe you can never learn it and just forget about the goal of attaining *effortlessness*, that is, to say, mentally throw in the towel.

What Is Talent?

"I simply don't have enough talent." This should be the first sentence that you strike from your list. This thought can be an enormous obstacle to your development. Thinking this way can lead you into finding yourself in a laborious struggle because you believe that only the really talented riders can reach the goal of melting into a harmonious unit with the horse. False! We can see this in a short look at another discipline. Matthew Syed, a world-class table-tennis professional from England, doesn't consider "talent" to be the highest contributor to his success. In his view "practice" is much more decisive. You can imagine the thousands of hours of practice that very many of the greats in sport and in the arts have spent before they arrive at fame and success.

I received a comment several years ago from a judge at a switch riding test that made me very happy. At this competition, young horses are judged while presented by their trainers then shown by other experienced riders who don't know that horse. The comment read: "You have a talent that I see only rarely. The horses want to work for you." So said the judge. Naturally, I like the complements about talent that I sometimes get from spectators or such experts. I don't give them much credence, however, as a decisive factor in success. I think the judge identified a much more important factor with his comment than the word "talent": intuitive understanding. In the switch-rider test, you sit a maximum of five minutes on the horse and how well you do depends on how fast you can understand him. That can happen more easily if you are born with that sensitivity.

But I practice it by riding many different horses every day, adjusting myself to every animal anew. What is talent and what is practice?

Matthew Syen considers 10 years and 10,000 hours of practice to be a suitable number as a basis for top performance. Syed supports his thesis with prominent examples: Mozart started "brutally" young practicing the piano and played much better than most adults when he officially emerged into the light of day. He had probably practiced more than 3500 hours before he was six years old. As a young man, he had already composed works, but his first masterwork, Concerto No. 9 for piano and orchestra was not finished until he was 21 years old.

The table-tennis pro Syed grew up in an area of the city where many supportive circumstances existed, which you could easily lump together as "talent." He puts this in perspective in this way. First, his father bought a competition-quality table-tennis table early on. Second, there was an open garage where they could *always* play. Third, his brother was equally obsessed and the sisters challenged them. Fourth, his coach encouraged table tennis so aggressively that many table-tennis professionals came out of that school. The result was that in the course of his career, Syed won all there was to win, but he never considered himself especially talented.

But what does this mean for our *effortless riding*? Nothing less than the good news: you can learn it as "normal" if you get the "no-talent" block out of your head. We can overcome this and other programs that we have been carrying around with us since we were children.

10 Years to Grand Prix—A Natural Talent?
by Friederike Heidenhof

Jasmin Simon on Dandelion.

Jasmin Simon, Uta's head groom and indispensable part of the team, began her training in breeding and horse care more than 10 years ago at Gut Rothenkircherhof. Since I arrived at Gut Rothenkircherhof, I have watched and been astounded at Jassi's equestrian development, which occurred in what I think is a perfect way. As a beginner, she had moderate riding instruction on not so good horses. After that, Jassi took a short cut with Uta. She didn't have to take the detour through "riding with effort" and lots of physical exertion, but was able to learn from Uta a sensitive way of riding with minimal aids right away. Compared with other riders she is actually a latecomer since she was already 13 before she had any contact with horses. At that time, she began to accompany her sister to a riding school. "When I needed to make a career decision, I thought about what could be more fun than riding and spending the whole day with horses. Nothing occurred to me," Jassi said, as she communicated her decision to live a life with horses. Her emphasis was less on riding and more on horse care. At Rothenkircherhof, it is typical for trainees, regardless of the direction in their training, to get pulled into riding. Jassi not only cares for the "good ones," but also rides horses like Le Noir, Damon Jerome NRW, and Dandelion. Mathew Syed's rule of thumb, "10 years and 10,000 hours," is appropriate for Jassi. Over the past 10 years she has so developed as a rider that she can ride the Grand Prix movements. She has no interest in competition, but she enjoys practicing every day. Her own special talent is that she never tires of working with horses and she has a high degree of intuitive understanding.

A riding student told me a funny story on the subject of "having to practice a lot in order to progress." I had wanted to encourage her 10-year-old son and said, "Watch out, in four weeks you will be so far along that you will be able to ride your horse through the poll." For some reason, he didn't ride for about two weeks, but said full of conviction to his mother, "Another two weeks, Uta said, and then my horse with be through the poll!" Apparently he thought diligent practice was unnecessary!

Mental Training Helps!

I am lucky in many ways. By nature, I am rather optimistic, easygoing, rarely nervous, relatively relaxed, and got a healthy degree of self-confidence along the way from my parents. I would also include patience and intuitive understanding. I believe these characteristics help me get along with horses and ride with little effort. I sometimes see mental blocks in my riding students and I focus then on "training the head." Sometimes, a rider gets impatient during the lesson and scolds the horse when something doesn't work right. At the same time, she totally tenses up and gets bogged down. Happily, I haven't experienced this myself. For someone who does, mental training can be helpful.

Friederike and I are big fans of Jane Savoie's "positive thinking equals successful riding," which she writes about in her books, such as *It's Not Just About the Ribbons*. We also discovered some interesting perspectives in a conversation with Gaby Bussmann, the sports psychologist for the German cadre of riders.

Mental training can keep one's own psyche from becoming a part of the problem and, thereby, losing the effortlessness in riding. It is a very broad subject. Consequently, we limit ourselves through mental blocks from achieving our desired effortless riding. We will try to show how we can overcome them.

An Anecdote in Passing
by Friederike Heidenhof

Those who know Uta Gräf or have watched her from afar, will agree with me that she goes through life a cheerful person. We have known each other for a long time and I can scarcely remember a time when she was in a bad mood. Since others also know of her gift of happiness, I would like to share the following funny scene that happened at the CHIO in Aachen. Uta was meeting with Gaby Bussmann, the sports psychologist for the German cadre of riders, to discuss her ideas about mental training. Two people who I didn't know were talking a little way away. One, who knew Uta well, asked: "Where is Uta?" The other answered: "She is sitting over there with Gaby Bussmann." Upon which the first commented: "Why? Does Gaby have a problem?"

From over-ambition to more composure. Extreme ambition can give us riders a mental block and send us in the wrong direction. More composure can help to put achieving the next training level into the background for a while and concentrating instead on refining what you have already achieved. Try to consciously pause and focus on riding the exercises and movements that you already do well with your horse—with less energy. Make calmness your next goal!

Think positively and realistically. It is a shame when someone can improve something in riding and becomes discontented. Perhaps that's because the next step isn't working yet while what you have already achieved is a great success in the scope of your own circumstances. Pessimists primarily see what they can't yet do in riding. They blame it on insufficient talent, the horse, the circumstances, and above all, they feel everything is against them. So how can they ride sensitively, harmoniously, and effortlessly? Even when a rider has consciously embraced the concept of effortlessness, the pessimist in her throws the whole intention overboard as soon as something doesn't work. It can help to turn the tables. Be thankful for what you have already achieved, especially that you are able to sit on a horse *at all* and ride—regardless of discipline and at what level. And what of it if you never progress another step? You have still achieved more than several billion other people who have never had the joy of riding—that's first of all. And second, why in the world shouldn't you progress? You just haven't done it yet! Therefore, continue to practice and trust that all will stay good and will get better. With such an optimistic attitude your continued effort will get much easier.

From stress to joy. Stressed riders get only limited enjoyment from their hobby. Of course, you can't always avoid job or personal stress, but it is better not to take it into the saddle with you. Riding is a brilliant stress killer because you automatically concentrate on the horse as soon as you ride off. But careful! Don't fall into the trap and make riding your next stressful experience by needing to do everything perfectly now.

It's enough for it to be better than yesterday and much better than many others can do it. Try to stay joyfully in the here and now. Enjoy walking outside in the summer evening sun. Consciously feel how beautiful it is to sit on the back of an animal and have the nice companionship of other horse lovers. Enjoy what you do and don't make it the next "problem box." Focus on the intention, right now, to do what you have already accomplished with less energy. Notice the small successes and be happy about them! Take breaks and praise your horse so that you share your joy of living with your horse.

From no drive to motivation. Let's say our horse is lazy, has no drive and is unmotivated. Can it be because we aren't bubbling over with motivation? We hope that dealing with a horse and riding will pull us out of the depths. But shouldn't it be the other way around too? By nature, it means nothing to the horse whether we ride him or not. So it is our job to offer the horse a program that is not demotivating but—in the best case—excites him, and to develop his enjoyment of working with us on a shared job. We have already quoted Monika Krämer, "Getting a horse to trot is not the same as motivating him." It doesn't promise much for success if we sit on the horse unhappy and mechanically drive him forward. That is exhausting for the rider as well as the horse. Krämer differentiates between "mobilize" and "motivate." In the former, every activity must be demanded, while with motivation, the effort is freely given. The art is in making the work so interesting for the horse that he finds it personally pleasant. Regarding our goal of effortlessness, this means that he who endeavors to ride a horse that responds to fine aids, should pay attention from the beginning that the horse offers the desired behavior almost by himself. According to Krämer, effortlessness can only come from motivation and not from obedience or avoidance of pain. Doesn't that make sense? *We* are the ones that must transfer our motivation to our horses, not the other way around. This opens the way to more effortlessness.

From technique to intuitive understanding: As discussed previously, many riders concentrate too much using the right technique. As in the example about Hannelore Brenner and the Journalist at the London Olympics (p. 45), many lay people believe that a harmonious ride comes from pushing the right buttons on the horse. We think this technical orientation has to end up in an arduous relationship. The idea of effortlessness is, in our experience, only possible with a high degree of intuitive understanding. As a rider, I have to be able to put myself in the thought process of the horse as a herd and flight animal and provide him with the neces-

We are doing together what we have dreamed of doing. Horses aren't stress. They are joy! Le Charmeur Noir, Stefan, and Uta.

Without motivation and fun, Xinoca couldn't express such effortlessness. Technique alone won't do it. Stefan on Xinoca.

"You can determine the shortcomings of your aids from the horse's reactions." — *Richard Hinrichs*

sary security. Then the horse can step back from scanning the surroundings for possible dangers and focus on me and our work. This helps the rider get away from thoughts controlling his horse and locking him into some type of frame. It is worth it to work on yourself and evolve from a technician to an empathetic rider who asks her horse how he is feeling and can put herself in his frame of mind.

From tension to relaxation. A furrowed brow, hectic running back and forth, a nervous fumbling with the saddle: this all smells of tension even before the rider has put a foot in the stirrup. Our advice, though not politically correct, is: drink a glass of wine and the world will look different! Since my single glass of champagne that I drink once a year at New Year's usually stays half full, I can say with a good conscience that there is another way. Let go, relax. Don't take everything so seriously.

This is easier said than done for people who weren't born with lightness. Your horse will better be able to let go himself when you sit comfortably on his back, relax and let go yourself. It also helps to think about your equestrian goals. Do I really have to reach the next level? Or, can I be happy with what I have already achieved? Once you are free of inner and outer tension, it is easier to give the horse breaks, praise him, and let him chew the reins out of the hand. Also, laughing liberates you. I can say this from my own experience, because we laugh a lot at our farm. We find a lot to be funny and we all have a good sense of humor. When there is happiness around, it is harder to sit with tension on the horse. Relaxation techniques like yoga, progressive muscle relaxation, or meditation can also be helpful. You can also include gymnastics and massage. Try them all!

Admittedly, relaxation is especially difficult for those riders who practice another profession and are still active in a competitive sport. I benefit from my profession giving me unbelievable fun. I am living my dream when I sit on one of my horses and

> "The maximum is not always the optimum."
> — *Richard Hinrichs*

We have a lot of fun with our team. We love telling jokes, watching funny You-Tube videos, or lifting ourselves up....

continue training Monday morning after a competition in streaming rain. In that moment, when I am totally engrossed in something, I feel no burden.

From doubts to self-confidence. Low self-confidence frequently causes riders to doubt themselves all too quickly. When I am teaching, I sometimes see riding students stopping an exercise, for example, leg-yield, three times in a row because the horse doesn't go sideways immediately. This can be caused by riders' insecurity because many are afraid of doing something wrong. Instead of resolutely completing the exercise and strengthening the sideways aids a little, doubt takes over. Am I using the correct aids? Shouldn't I be doing it differently? The horse learns from such situations: "Ah ha! If I don't go sideways, my rider makes me more comfortable." When you repeat this a couple times, the learning effect is reinforced and the leg-yield takes much longer and is more difficult to teach. Therefore, only attempt goals that are realistic to achieve. Then you can consciously set your doubt aside and complete what you have begun, not half-heartedly, but with conviction—not with a sledgehammer but within the bounds of what can be achieved. You can then decide if you were successful or not.

Work with Mental Images

At a seminar in Reken, Richard Hinrichs said to the audience, "Horses are telepathic." Disbelieving astonishment dissolved into nods of agreement as the expert on fine and effortless riding continued to explain what he meant by that. "The horse should respond to the inner picture and the thoughts of the rider. That is, if the rider has clear thoughts!" Then, Hinrichs made the point that everyone understood: we riders are all too often part of the problem when riding is difficult.

> "The horse can respond to the mental image and the thoughts of the rider.
> That is, if the rider has clear thoughts!"
> — *Richard Hinrichs*

Perhaps we get frustrated when an exercise or lesson isn't successful. But if we are honest, maybe we have only vaguely thought in advance about what we want to ride. Do you simply start a serpentine and see how many loops you end up with? When riding the changes on the diagonal, do you think, "I am able to do four-tempis well, so okay, I will ride fours." But how many? As many as will fit?

Hinrichs emphasizes that we should have in advance a precise mental image of what we are going to accomplish by the end of the exercise. He says about himself, "Whenever something doesn't go well, I catch myself not giving precise commands."

Making his thoughts more precise, for example, with serpentines would mean, "I want to ride four-loop serpentines at the trot without losing swing, reach to the hand or tempo. The serpentine loops should be the same size and my horse shall change the bend in the new direction across the centerline."

For flying changes on the diagonal, precision of thoughts means, "I want five consecutive four-stride flying changes. My horse should jump through with expression and the poll should stay up."

Hinrichs advises making the mental image more concrete and stronger, "It's like with a good fairy: if my wish is not well formulated, I get the opposite!" And he continues, "Horses understand more than you think—even negative thoughts."

That is why it is especially important to formulate your mental images to the positive: "The poll should stay up during flying changes." is more positive than, "My horse shouldn't dive down."

> "Like a wish to a good fairy: if it isn't well formulated,
> you will get the opposite!"
> — *Richard Hinrichs*

I have had "Aha!" experiences from some of the images out of Jane Savoie's book *It's Not Just About the Ribbons!* For example, I like the image of the cone of concentration. Savoie advises competition riders to imagine as they ride into the test arena that they are under a cone that shields them from all external influences. Read it once and remember forever! The usefulness of this image was clear when a dressage friend told me that while riding in the neighboring arena, she overheard that someone prominent had just ridden a zero round. Nothing more. But that was enough to distract her for the next several meters. And in the Grand Prix, there can be five things happening in a few meters. The cone would have helped her for sure! I heard a funny comment from another rider that I told about the cone. She said, "I was under the cone for the whole test! Unfortunately, I forgot to take my horse under it with me."

Another helpful mental image of Savoie's is the centaur: a muscular man without legs whose midsection merges into a horse with whom he is as one. It's a horse

> "We shouldn't get stuck in mediocrity. That goes for riding as well as in life!"
> — *Richard Hinrichs*

with a human upper body. Savoie recommends this picture as an example of how it should feel to become one with the horse in full harmony and to ride effortlessly.

Mental images help bring us a step closer to effortless riding, because they help us be more precise in our request for what we want.

When I set out to work with mental images, I train myself to visualize with my inner eye what I want to achieve. Achieving state of flow in an exercise, while jumping or while trail riding is the ultimate. By this, I mean the feeling of being completely absorbed in the activity. In a video that Ingrid Klimke took with her helmet camera during her ride at Luhmühlen, she whispers in several places, "Now just enjoy the ride!" She seems to be in the flow—perhaps comparable to a pianist while fingers fly over the keys while lost in thought. Ingrid Klimke rides consciously to every single obstacle, but in the video the watcher gets the impression that the whole run just *happens*. Just like the pianist who doesn't read every individual note anymore when he plays a complex piece.

I, too, have experienced being in the flow while training and also at competitions. For example, I remember the Grand Prix freestyle in Wiesbaden in 2012, which went especially well. Everything was right. It was a soft summer night, the audience greeted us in a friendly way and Le Noir was in top form. I had the feeling of being taken along by the horse, giving him minimal aids as to what we were going to ride next. It was pure joy. During the test I thought to myself, "Today everything is working." And so it was. I still love watching this test on DVD, and I remember the sensational feeling and the equally sensational triumph in the test!

Useful Tips for Mental Images for Effortless Riding

Effortless trot extensions. As I begin the extension it helps me to think of a horse that is especially good at trot extensions. Try thinking about Damon Hill as he comes across the diagonal in an extended trot!

Effortless cross-country canter stretches. Likewise, thinking of how Ingrid Klimke rides cross-country can help you take her secure and unflappable feeling along with you in the saddle.

Effortless pirouette. Even with horses that aren't trained this far, I imagine the feeling of sitting on Le Noir or Dandelion and riding the pirouette with fine aids. This helps me get the feeling on other horses.

Effortless good seat. Likewise, it can be helpful to have rider examples in your mind. How Ingrid Klimke holds her hands is a good model that can help you keep your hands quiet, not carry them too high, and carry them independently from your body.

Maybe you think that these are all ideals that you can't achieve. That's true. We heard from Matthew Syed that he estimates that it takes about 10,000 practice hours and 10 years to approach perfection in any discipline. And, how in heaven are we supposed to achieve the desired goal if we don't have the goal for which we strive pictured in our mind? So, this is our tip. Mentally run through every exercise that you and your horse have in your repertoire. Imagine, or even write out, what perfect execution would be. It is highly likely that you will have internalized it by the next practice session. I would be disappointed if this didn't take you at least a little way in the right direction.

Jane Savoie, author and successful dressage rider, recommends to her readers that they visualize the execution of exercises to improve them. For example, to improve leg-yields, you should mentally zoom in on the hind legs of the horse. Visualize your horse clearly crossing the legs like in a film. Savoie explains to readers that you maintain the image while you ride the leg-yields, not just so that your own muscles respond to the picture, but also so the horse gets a clear picture of what you want from him. Her Olympic horse Zapatero always did a correct piaffe when she visualized the rhythmical stepping precisely. As soon as your thoughts stray, your mind goes blank. Visualizing can also work in the negative direction. If I think too much about how my horse is going to shy at a garbage sack in a bush, then that is highly likely to happen.

The Courage to Be Lazy

What? Laziness can bring us closer to effortless riding? Right! Set out to be bone idle, to put it mildly, for the next 500 of the necessary 10,000 practice hours. Start with getting on. Does your horse stay standing still? It causes you effort trying to get on when your horse is more comfortable simply moving off. If you want to be lazy while getting on in the future, you have to make it clear to your horse *right now* that he must stay standing still. While walking, do you have to *drive* every step out of your horse? That uses energy before you have even really begun to ride. But you want to be lazy. You should expect your horse to move off in an energetic walk —*right now*—so that you can be lazy while walking forever, because from now on you rarely want to think about being active, if at all. How else are you going to be able to *drink coffee*? The same goes for the posting trot. Do you have to keep your horse going for every step? That may have been okay—until today. From today on, *you* are lazy and your horse maintains the trot on his own. This gives you the chance to enjoy the trot and let him carry you. Can you remember this?

Perhaps you still object, "That is unheard of! Wanting to be lazy on a horse!" And you are right, because to achieve your goal you can't be completely lazy. Changing how you ride requires analysis of the subject of effortlessness along with energetic and single-minded practice. It doesn't mean just sitting up there and doing nothing. "The courage to be lazy" is an exaggeration that is helpful because you want to finally do everything you have achieved so far with less effort. You should be especially active in these areas: give aids in pulses instead of constantly, notice when it is good and relax, enable the horse to find his own balance, develop mental images, reflect, and think things through.

> "Take the trouble now to ride effortlessly in the future—
> that is how we can sum it up!"
>
> — *Uta Gräf*

Dandelion—Journal of a Newcomer (2)
More "Courage to Be Lazy"

I am increasingly able to explore "more courage to be lazy," even with Dandelion. Because Dandelion previously learned pirouettes from an experienced trainer, I didn't have a lot to do there. It was a good experience and I could internalize more how a good pirouette feels. Dandelion is a strong horse in a positive sense. He has an enormous talent for the exercises that require a lot of power, like pirouettes, piaffe, and passage.

CHALLENGES: Although we had already achieved many wins at the S level (Fourth Level/Prix St. Georges) of dressage, the main issue to work on was relaxation. Tempi changes stressed him for a long time before they gradually got easier. Now he likes to do them, but maybe he always wants to do too well?

TRAINING PROGRAM FOR 10- AND 11-YEAR-OLD: We have begun piaffe and passage and prepared him for his first attempts at Grand Prix. Dandelion didn't like me driving with my calves in the piaffe. I got better at using the whip to help him a little with the rhythm. His piaffe improved when I used very little leg aid. Whips aren't allowed at the international-level tests, which we don't plan on entering until later, so I have to change the aid sooner or later.

RESULT: Dandelion had his first start in Grand Prix at the national level as an 11-year-old. He regularly brought home yellow ribbons from the first few starts. The likeable gelding had blossomed into a newcomer on the Grand Prix scene!

Dandelion

Just Breathe Deeply

Being able to relax yourself is one of the most important aspects along the way to effortless riding. Previously, we have thoroughly explored how important it is to alternate between pulsing aids and relaxation (p. 9). It doesn't work as well when I breathe shallowly or hold my breath. Good breathing technique is very helpful for a harmonious connection melting into the horse. Many don't know how they are breathing while they ride. I didn't think about it much myself until I ran across the image of the centaur already mentioned. The centaur has a human upper body merged into the horse's body so the human is at one with the horse.

One of our favorite authors, Jane Savoie, gives this advice:

Practice abdominal breathing to be a centaur while you ride. Breathe in through the nose with the feeling of pumping the air deep down into your abdomen. Your belly should extend out as if you want to be as fat as possible. Then breathe out slowly through the mouth and feel your seat muscles relax so that you don't feel perched on the horse or disconnected from the horse but rather feel like one unit with the horse. Imagine that your seat melts into the horse's body until you act like a centaur. Breathe consciously in this way when you mount and repeat this breathing process in segments throughout the practice session and every time when you come to a walk.

Deep breathing promotes relaxation that is picked up by the horse in all circumstances. On a trail ride, deep breathing can help me overcome a scary situation because the horse notices that his rider has everything under control. At a competition, I can help the next movement by overcoming test anxiety. Try to remember to wait a second longer to breathe in and out deeply while at the initial salute.

To achieve a feeling of unity with the horse, consciously breathe in deeply into the abdomen. Uta with Le Noir.

Le Noir's eagerness and joy in moving are ideal for Uta's goal of effortlessness.

Wait another second until your horse also takes a deep breath. Don't lose your nerve—it will come! Afterward, the world of the dressage arena will look completely different and you can begin the test more relaxed.

What Fits? About Human and Horse Types

What causes us trouble depends essentially on what stresses us. Strenuous effort is a question of personal perception. It would be extremely difficult for me to work in an office job, day in and day out. For others, it would be exhausting to ride outside in wind and bad weather. For me, that is not a problem because I love what I do, and it is simply part of it to work outside in nature. Horses are just as much individuals as we are in our perceptions.

To have a trouble-free partnership, the nature of the horse should ideally match what the rider finds pleasant. I, for example, like horses that are energetic rather than the more laid-back types. I prefer riding a horse when I can feel his joy in moving and eagerness. Consequently, it isn't trouble for me to patiently bring such a horse back to the right tempo and help him find more relaxation. For me, it is much more effort to have to push on a lazy horse because I feel he doesn't have the desire to train with me.

We can save ourselves a lot of trouble in the saddle if we know our own preferences, tendencies, and characteristics and keep these in mind when we select a horse. Frequently, this aspect is not given enough regard because many other

When rider and horse fit together, contentment radiates from them both. Uta with Le Noir.

factors are stronger influences on the purchase decision, such as ability, stage of training, size, color, health, and more.

In our business, I experience daily what a difference it makes when the horse and rider fit each other mentally and in basic characteristics. We have on average four to five colleagues as well as a whole array of horse types. It is my job to figure out who fits which horse the best. All the riders have a certain riding horse they are primarily responsible for, along with me. For example, there was a large bay that was a stallion until he was five. I had two people who rode equally well that I was considering for him. One of them loved this stallion with all his special characteristics. For her, it was the best part of the day to get to ride him. The second rider found the bay to be difficult. If I had made the wrong choice, she wouldn't have been happy with the horse, and rider and horse would have found the work together to be troublesome. Likewise, the first person would have lost a great deal of her daily joy if she hadn't been able to ride that horse.

As for the rider, so the horse: for example, horses ridden by tense, cramped riders tend to be "sticky." Nervous people quickly make sensitive horses jumpy and insecure. Sensitive people can scarcely get started with horses that are bullies, while calm riders usually do well with hyperactive dynamos. A nervous horse ridden by a nervous rider usually doesn't work. We shouldn't undervalue this reciprocal relationship and should notice when buying a horse what stresses the horse and the human. When I am looking to buy a horse I still think about this aspect. After the purchase, it can be difficult to find a common wavelength. What do you do when you determine afterward that some characteristic of your horse in combination with your own stress pattern complicates riding?

Now to the *timid* types: to correctly handle a *fearful* horse, the rider needs to give him security. And, a fearful rider needs a horse that she can trust. And the *hyperactive* ones: a horse with an exaggerated desire to move needs sufficient turnout, a job, social contact, and training. Changing how this horse is cared for and trained can achieve a lot. It can be helpful to have him ridden initially by someone that isn't bothered as much by his hectic nature until he is a little calmer. An additional program on leading, groundwork and longeing can also help. It is similar for the *hot horse*. An experienced, calm rider is ideal, however, an insecure or fearful rider is definitely not the right one. An especially *sensitive horse* is not appropriate for a rider that feels more comfortable on a horse that can just ignore her riding errors. A sensitive rider loses her confidence on a *thick-skinned horse* that causes her a lot of effort to make go forward well, while another rider might be glad not to have to rein in a horse that is too dynamic. Under certain circumstances, a horse that behaves "loutishly" with bad manners, quickly gets on the nerves of a rider who is correct and well-organized.

On the other hand, the low-key horse is trouble for the sensitive rider.

A Variety of Horses—It Matters for the Professional

by Friederike Heidenhof

Experience is best developed by riding many different horses. Franziska Aumer on the training horse Lexington.

Conversations with Uta about different aspects of a certain subject are among the most interesting things involved in the development of our books. As an amateur rider with a lot of years with horses, I am always fascinated by the fact that for every facet there is also another point of view. What sets Uta and other professionals apart is that they have very broad experience they can call on from riding a large number of different types of horses. As a result, she knows with which horse she must make certain compromises at first, and for which horse that would be "deadly" because it would lead to insecurity and unintended consequences. A broad mixture of horses makes it possible to work through problems and challenges in a given circumstance, while a one-horse amateur would be quicker to get into trouble. A professional is also generally much more likely to be able to understand different horse personalities and to control her own state of mind. Therefore, it is helpful for amateurs to ride different horses from time to time. Especially sensitive horses can be made insecure by an unknown rider while others could enjoy being ridden in a different way. Riding a horse that doesn't have the characteristic that is a problem for us with our own horses can strengthen our self-confidence and bring new joy to the subject.

At the beginning, Dandelion was somewhat timid and I was able to give him security and trust. Since we fit well together, I was glad that Dandelion was able to stay in our program because the owner of another horse we have in training wanted to buy him. "And what if he doesn't progress very far?" I asked up front to make clear that we couldn't guarantee that her new horse would be as successful as we all hoped. Something can go wrong. "He will never be sold. I would just ride him on the trail," said his new owner and she really meant it even though she would never buy such a gifted horse for that purpose.

But she had already fallen for the pretty bay a long time ago. We were happy: horse, rider, and owner fit perfectly together. He did go on trails, but the day that trail riding would become his main occupation was, we hoped, many years away.

I don't know exactly what goes on in a horse when he first steps into Schleyer Hall in Stuttgart. In his first Grand Prix test in 2013, Dandelion was so excited that we made some errors. He seemed anxious and insecure. The next day was the Grand Prix Special. In the second go, I suddenly felt Dandelion's self-confidence return. To be sure, every time we went around, he looked at the newly hung advertisements on the rail, but inside he had gathered himself. It was clear to me that we could give him more security and self-confidence if we continued to practice patiently. At home, we put up our own makeshift signs on the wall so that Dandelion could practice staying on the track even when things that worried him were hanging there. We made a positive impression at Stuttgart and we wanted to own it. Shortly before Christmas, there was going to be a big competition in Frankfurt. To make it brief, Dandelion got progressively more relaxed. In Frankfurt, he stood his ground well in both Grand Prix tests against a strong group of competitors. The "country bumpkin" had turned into a real looker that needed just a little more time to overcome his timidity.

Practicing with wall signs helps Dandelion...

...to overcome his timidity.

Uta and Lexington

Easygoing Through the Test!

Effortless Riding Even in Competition

The Relaxed Way to Success

"Passion wins"—this is a saying of recognized sports psychologists that I absolutely agree with. I am convinced that it is critical whether what I do or want to achieve is done out of passion or out of duty. When an activity is fun for us, it gives us energy. If not, it costs us energy and effort. Do you know the feeling of forgetting about the effort when you are working on your favorite pastime?

Passion wins. What is fun doesn't require effort. Uta with Le Noir's owners Hans and Christiane Herzog.

My favorite thing to do is ride. I enjoy sitting on horses and having a dreamlike feeling because I can build unity with this fascinating creature. It doesn't cost an ounce of effort for me. As long as I am interacting with horses, I am in my element, regardless of whether it is cold or hot, raining or the sun is shining. It also isn't so bad when there is a lot to do in the barn or I get home late from a competition. I can't find this state of effortlessness with any other activity because I don't have the same enthusiasm for any other activity other than riding. My chosen profession was actually a detour. While I was waiting for a place at university, I supported myself riding. I noticed that my joy of riding wasn't lessened by having to do it to make money. That was always very important to me, because I never

Uta with Damon Jerome NRW's owner Prof. Dr. Thomas Hitschold.

would have come so far without loving riding. I also have fun in our joint successes with the horse owners. Consequently, it was the best decision of my life to do what really gives me joy and about which I can be so enthusiastic.

What does this have to do with effortless riding at a competition? A lot. If you don't enjoy competitions then you will easily find them difficult. If you feel competing is an obligation, for whatever reason, then I ask, why don't you just leave it alone? No rider in the world *must* compete when it overly stresses and frustrates her. If riding is your passion, just not competition, the simplest recipe for less effort in riding is to not compete. For me, riding in competition is fantastic and exciting. I love it when I set a challenge for my horse and me, and prepare for it perfectly. In this way, my own measurements stay in the foreground and not the expectations of everyone else. I don't worry about competing because I feel obligated first of all to myself. This mental freedom is important to me, because I take it with me into the test. If you like to ride in competitions and wish to know how even there you can achieve more effortlessness, the following tips might help you.

Let the Horse Think Things Through—Even in the Arena

From the beginning, a young horse should be motivated to think things through in the test. Then it doesn't just look effortless, it is! Uta with Lexington.

It is important to allow the horse to think things through to reduce stress in the test arena. Under competitive conditions, it is even more important to understand each other almost blind in order to perform the sequences you have easily worked on together. The table-tennis pro Matthew Syed has an example for us. He describes getting in a state where the movements are intuitively coordinated and unconsciously called forth in the process of returning lightning fast balls. As previously stated, he had won everything there was to win in world-class table tennis, until the 1992 Olympics in Sydney. His career was at an end and he wanted to win a medal at any cost. In the decisive game, he totally failed. His equally skilled opponent won hands down as if he had been playing against a representative of the local old-fogies team. What happened? The pressure was too great, he started thinking. The effortlessness of his very agile motion and split-second reactions was all suddenly lost and he couldn't do it anymore.

It is the same with riding. The fine-tuning with the horse unfolds unconsciously under competition conditions, thanks to many years of practice and learning to work together with horses. If I start wanting to overly control my horse in the test, my feeling of effortlessness in the test goes down the river. But it is my goal to enjoy the ride. If I can enjoy myself during the test, it will be good. I also want to ride the test with as little energy as possible. For that to be possible, my horse must think things through. Like Ingrid Klimke wrote in her column, I introduce the exercise and the horse carries it out, just as we do at home. I have to give the horse, even in the test, a certain amount of independence, not squeezing him into a frame and not requiring push-button punctuality of the movements. Even in a test, the horse can be strengthened in his courage and self-trust so that he radiates his full personality and beauty. I strive to ride my horses in the test with the nose in front of the vertical and the poll as the highest point. Like Ingrid Klimke in cross-country, the horses need to be able to see to think things through and work with you. In large halls with a lot of spectators, the horse needs a lot of self-assurance and courage. We must not take this away through over control. Their full potential and nobility unfolds, and I would risk losing that if I threw my principles overboard—just because it is a competition.

Dandelion—Journal of a Newcomer (3)

Courage and Self-Assurance Grow!

It actually wasn't planned to show Dandelion in international Grand Prix tests in 2013. We had just begun to get rid of the whip in piaffe. Due to a break in Le Noir's competition schedule, we took Dandelion on the Big Tours earlier than planned, namely to Balve for the German Championships. At first sight, the atmosphere was like a big jump into cold water for him. After Balve came the CHIO in Aachen. He had big shoes to fill. The country boy goes to Aachen. Who would have thought…?

TRAINING PROGRAM FOR A 12-YEAR-OLD: We haven't changed our training much, just patiently continuing to work on staying relaxed, even in difficult movements. Given the "no-whip" rule in international Grand Prix, Dandelion and my leg had to learn to get along for better or worse, even in piaffe.

RESULT: At the 2013 German Championships in Balve, Dandelion managed to place in the top ten and, thereby, automatically joined Le Noir in the German B-team of dressage. He was also allowed to show shortly afterward at Aachen and averaged 74 percent after the trot tour. He made a big jump during piaffe and the scores dropped. The score for relaxation had a lot of air above it, too. Nevertheless, the result was good and we were happy that we could expect much more out of this good horse!

Uta with Dandelion in Frankfurt.

Dandelion

Resilience—The Secret to Emotional Strength

In order to progress with a newcomer like Dandelion who isn't quite confirmed in everything like an old hand, you have to be able to cope with not being high in the ribbons. Maintaining effortlessness in a competitive situation requires staying steadfast regardless of external influence. For many riders, competitions and test situations are pure stress. Some people have more resistance to stress than others and can benefit from the increased tension. This has a lot to do with positive thinking, as we have already discussed in the chapter on mental training (p. 150). But that is just one aspect. Psychologists label the secret power of these people *resilience*—a resistance that encompasses calmness and self-confidence.

Christine Berndt describes a poignant picture in her book *Resilience—The Secret of Mental Resistance*: "There are people who have a type of 'callus' over their soul. They have an attitude toward life that directs their gaze optimistically forward and enables them to better cope with all kinds of challenges. There are some resilient types that don't despair after hard knocks of fate, and are optimistic again after a bit of time and remain positive their entire life."

Natascha Kampusch is a prominent example of this. As a 10-year-old she was abducted and held prisoner for years in a basement dungeon. As a young woman she gave the impression in her first interview after being rescued that she actually grew from her fate. Or Samuel Koch, who is paralyzed from the neck down after an accident and sits in a wheelchair, now shares his new start with a broad audience by talking and answering questions on television talk shows. And also our para-equestrians who don't despair over their handicap, but rather try to make the most of the opportunities that come to them.

When I reflect on such people, a little riding test seems a little laughable. I can get a comparatively thick skin when I look at something I am doing with a little more distance and think about it differently. Matthew Syed mentions the example of Sarah Lindsey, an Olympic speed skater who said to herself at the sight of a stadium with 27,000 spectators: "It's nothing more than speed skating!" When I ride into the test arena, I like to say, "It is just riding," then the test at a high level in front of a lot of people loses a lot of its potential terror.

Effortless riding in the test arena requires me to have an optimistic frame of mind.

There is a thing called the *self-fulfilling prophecy*. By this is meant that things happen precisely because someone believes they will happen. If you believe that a horse is going to shy somewhere, then it *will* shy there. Many people start sneezing only because they know that their neighbor is coming down with the flu. The classic book by Norman Vincent Peale from the 1950s, entitled *The Power of Positive Thinking*, says a lot just in the title. Faith in success is enormously important. A degree of frustration tolerance is helpful to build resistance to stress. If some-

thing doesn't go right, it is better to learn something positive from it rather than ending up doubting everything about how you ride. I personally don't see it as a problem when something goes wrong even if I was well prepared, as long as the error doesn't occur because we have mismanaged the ride. But, of course, that can happen too.

Matthew Syed recommends you maintain a certain reserve of attention under competition circumstances so that you can quickly forget about mistakes. If I focus all my concentration on a mistake already made, I have no synapses free to cope with the rest of the test effortlessly. Syed gives the following example on this subject: in the seventies, a plane crashed on the way to Miami because both pilots were talking about a broken warning light without noticing that they had mistakenly shut off the autopilot. Absorbed in discussion, they ignored even the altitude warning signal and noticed only when they were 15 feet above the ground that something was wrong. It was too late and 101 people died.

The power of positive thinking: Uta with Dandelion before riding into the CHIO stadium in Aachen. With a smile—it is only riding!

If I brood too long during the test about why the flying changes weren't successful this time, it is guaranteed that the pirouette that comes later won't be ridden effortlessly. I won't have the time to prepare the movement well. If my thoughts are still with the changes we messed up, I will lose some seconds and it will be too late to recover when I get to the location for the pirouette. I would surprise my horse with the next movement. He might get it halfway done, but not effortlessly and harmoniously.

Emergency Measures in the Test

There are situations within a test that can lead to the rest of the test not going well. When training at home, I can correct an exercise at any time or repeat it when an error occurs. The difficulty in riding tests is that all the movements come sequentially with similar speed. There is little time to get the horse correctly on the aids if he loses rhythm, swing, collection, or positioning and bend. Between the movements, the rider must make the horse supple again, engage the hindquarters, and put the horse in front of the leg. It is smart to think through where in the test and how to respond if worse comes to worst.

Let's be clear again about the toolbox for effortless and effective training. With transitions, changes of tempo, and changes of direction on bending lines, I can correct my horse in many situations. In the test, however, that obviously isn't possible. Or is it? Yes, it can work if I change my thinking a little. The movements weren't thought up just to give spectators a pretty picture. It is a good thing to consider that a particular movement isn't done to look good but rather to create a training effect. In the test, for example, a volte is required before the half-pass. Perfect. I use the volte, just like a correction in training, to develop position and bend and improve the activity and swing I already have. Then I go into the half-pass. Thanks to the preparation, I can better flow effortlessly into the lateral movement without having to drive the horse. That is an approach with only minimal changes, but it is more helpful than thinking: "Oh $#@*! I will lose the swing in the volte and my horse will get stuck in the half-pass that follows."

Another example: an extended trot on the diagonal is required right at the beginning of the test. This is difficult for many riders because they are afraid their horse will fall apart right at the beginning, and they won't be able to collect him for the rest of the test. However, if I think about it as a training exercise or correction exercise then it goes like this: "In training, I practice changes of tempo to collect my horse and to improve throughness. I can use the trot extension for the same purpose."

If engagement is still a problem, I ask a little less of the horse. I pay more attention to the fact that I can only ride out of my horse what my horse can bring from back to front to the hand, while carrying himself and staying in front of the aids, so that I can begin the following shoulder-in with an engaged horse. The shoulder-in is therefore, an opportunity to improve throughness for the exercises that follow.

So when we speak of emergency measures, it's not just to use the two meters in the corner to correct everything that has been lost. You can do that too, but it is more about using a movement itself as the preparation for the effortless riding of the next movement. That has an even greater advantage. During the current movement I am thinking about the next movement. From this point of view, dressage riders can learn something from jumping riders "after the jump is before the jump." I would change this saying to "after the movement is before the movement!"

Tips for a Feeling of Effortlessness in the Test

Allow the horse to think things through. During the test, adhere to the principle of having an independent horse that thinks things through with you. If you have practiced in advance having your horse wait for your aids, and if you introduce the movement and the horse independently executes the exercise, you have an enormous advantage.

Establish an emergency plan. Go systematically through the exercises that you are going to ride. What is easy for you and your horse? What can you use to prepare for other movements? Prepare an emergency plan for the whole test.

Block out external influences. Think about the image of the cone of concentration (see p. 140) as you ride in, and block out the audience as well as possible external pressures and expectations. It is only you, your horse, and your own expectations that you are obligated to.

Minimize the importance. It is only a test! Put what you are doing in a larger context, gain distance.

Quickly forget errors. Later there will be enough time to analyze mistakes. Don't block all your attention reserves with an immediate error analysis.

Enjoy and be thankful. Enjoy having a lovely experience together with your horse. Be thankful that you can have this experience at all.

Today I will ride the pirouette with DJ as effortlessly as with Le Noir! If it happens, drink coffee?

I am concentrating on what I want for the test and not on what I am afraid of.

(Tip from Jane Savoie on the power of positive thinking.)

DJ's trot is fantastic today. It feels like riding an ocean wave (to use Jane Savoie's metaphor in *It's Not Just About the Ribbons*).

It is super that I can start Damon Jerome here in Aachen. It is a wonderful feeling and I am thankful for it.

I'm loving the impulsion today. It was brilliant in the warm-up arena!

I imagine Jane Savoie's Cone of Concentration and can block everything out around me.

(see p. 140)

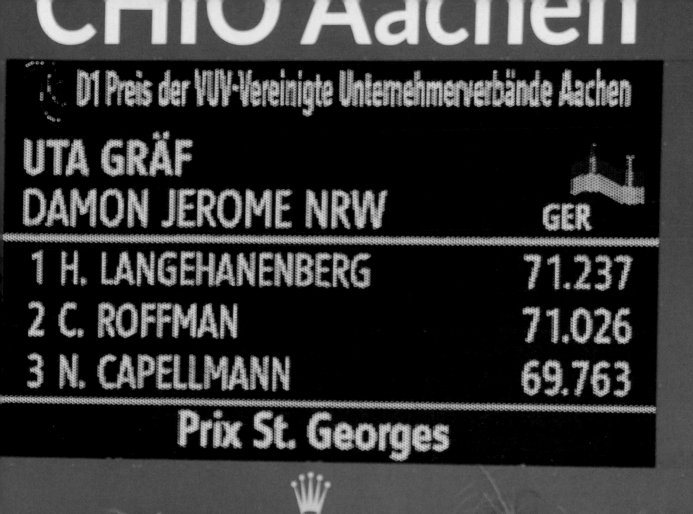

CHIO Aachen

D1 Preis der VUV-Vereinigte Unternehmerverbände Aachen

UTA GRÄF
DAMON JEROME NRW   **GER**

1	H. LANGEHANENBERG	71.237
2	C. ROFFMAN	71.026
3	N. CAPELLMANN	69.763

Prix St. Georges

ROLEX

My rider seems to be very relaxed.
That feels good. I don't have to worry.
Damon Jerome NRW

*Uta with Damon
Jerome NRW at CHIO
in Aachen 2013.*

The Finale

Effortless and Effective— Has the Goal Been Reached?

Achieving your own personal goal doesn't necessarily depend on success in the show ring. Our primary goal was and is to progress with the horse toward effort-lessness in riding and interacting with the horse. Ideally, the progress will translate to shows and end in success—if that is my goal. Our Journal horses have all made individual progress that we want to look at again in closing. It is often the little things that count and are more important than a sensational placing. Of course, we like achieving success, but we enjoy the improvements in effortlessness that are likely invisible to others. Now back to our horses. We begin with Dino, our Journal horse—the "not-so-perfect" gray gelding that brought with him a whole list of issues to work on.

Dino: Sniffing at St. George

Dino is now 12 years old and has developed further than we thought possible at the beginning. The original issues are still challenges, but we notice distinct progress. He engages much more dynamically from behind to the hand, re-laxes better in the poll, swings well over the back, and feels good at the trot. The lightness phase will take longer, but it is beginning. The jump in the canter has improved but is still a weakness. Since Dino is with us only part of the time, I advised Friederike to use the pastures at home in the Rheinland to really let Dino go at the canter while still keeping him engaged to create more push

for the dressage work. As always, the horse is a lot of fun for Friederike and she is convinced that Dino is the perfect horse for her. Through systematic training, Dino has come so far from his not-so-perfect original condition that Friederike has seized the opportunity to dare entering class M and Prix St. Georges dressage tests on her own. She commented, "As expected, the result was average and there were some errors. But we gave it a try and didn't do a complete nosedive. The test sheet showed definite areas for improvement and not just with the movements. I wasn't always able to accomplish in the test what we can do in training. We didn't really achieve effortlessness! But, we hold on to the quote from Goethe: 'One should rare-ly despair over impossible things, and never over what's difficult!'"

"Daily Soap" with Helios!

Helios became a "docu-star" over night because we took him to a few FN seminars for members where he was filmed. He was used as an example of how much you can achieve with a horse of average ability. To increase the audience to this training opportunity, we decided to publish the film in short clips on the Facebook page of Pferdia TV. We were able to show watchers that Helios needed a certain amount of time to relax and stretch to the hand under new circumstances. Over the course of a half-hour, he illustrates in time-lapsed photography the training process he has undergone to develop effortlessness, connection, impulsion, power, and swing. After the warm-up, Helios was well in front of the leg and traveled powerfully with a lot of expression in good connection. Now he didn't look so much like an "average" horse and many a spectator thought perhaps, *"Yeah, if he is an average horse, what does a super horse look like?"* The audience couldn't know that Helios had just

"Daily Soap" with Helios on Facebook Pferdia TV.

developed in the past few years to the horse that he is today, a talented dressage horse with potential for Grand Prix. From inclusion in the seminars, we learned that it made sense for Helios to enter some competitions during the next season to make it more routine for him so that he could maintain effortlessness under different circumstances. We penciled him in for the upcoming competitions in the spring and continued to train as normal.

DJ: On the Way to the Class of Kings

Damon Jerome NRW is now nine years old and is confirmed in all the S movements (Fourth Level/Prix St. Georges). On a scale from 1 to 10 (for maximal effortlessness in training), DJ scores a 9.8 in my personal opinion. But our experience at the finale of the Nurnberg Burgpokal in Frankfurt showed that even such a horse can be irritated and have trouble performing in the test what he can do so well at home. But that didn't mean for us that we hadn't reached our goal for effortless riding, because we hadn't had 100 percent of all the success we wanted. DJ had a very successful season and we could conclude that his training could continue effortlessly. After the end of the competition season we declared a winter break. Since DJ characteristically is a horse that likes to work, he wants to be busy and challenged. After the break, we used the rest of the winter to work in the direction of Grand Prix. We are happy every day to have such a fantastic horse at the barn.

At home DJ is a quiet and calm stallion because we rarely have mares at Gut Rothenkircherhof. But the situation changes when our man finds himself relatively close to the other sex in competition barns. Thanks to Stefan's groundwork, he was always good to handle and ride, but we could sense his increasing discomfort, especially at night in the stall. At several competitions, DJ had scarcely a minute's rest. He walked around and around in the stall instead of having his well-deserved sleep. At this time, we began to think that DJ's life would be easier if he didn't have to spend every night at the show. Since gelding a stallion is an irreversible decision, we dropped the thought as soon as the situation at competitions faded in our memory. One day the penny dropped for us and for DJ's owners. It was suddenly clear that it was the right time. It was summer, the herd was out in the meadow and we fully understood how much good it would do Damon Jerome NRW to be with his barn buddies, jumping over the stream, and across the huge meadow at a full gallop. It all happened quickly and DJ recovered from the operation in a few days. We now are all glad to watch how happily he plays with the boys instead of staring at unreachable mares.

We also much enjoyed his first Grand Prix because now he could recover during the night from the day's competition.

Dandelion: All Issues Gone!

After the working with signs on the sidewalls of the arena that we started after the Stuttgart show, we continued to work patiently on Dandelion's relaxation. We felt this was the essential key to effortlessness at a show. We have also improved the fine-tuning of his flying changes and piaffe, even though Dandelion can still get hot.

The 2014 Grand Prix in Münster was right at the beginning of the year and was in our plan. We decided to start the gelding there because he was in top form in training. He was increasingly more relaxed and the piaffe kept getting better. He now accepted my leg well and his piaffe was very engaged and expressive without a whip. Dandelion's pirouttes were of "coffee-drinking" quality from the beginning. The challenge now was to finish exactly according to our goal, to make everything we had achieved up to now still more effortless. Münster was the high point for Dandelion. The signs on the rail didn't overly irritate him and he wasn't particularly excited in the arena. Our desensitization training had definitely paid off. With over 76 percent, the judges unanimously placed our bay first in the Grand Prix Special.

The success streak didn't break. Two months later, Dandelion was second at Dortmund in the international level Grand Prix freestyle and won an international Grand Prix Special for the first time in Mannheim. We were almost a little over-whelmed because we know how timid our little Dandelion is. But his heart was big enough for the Grand Prix on the big stage! We had clearly achieved his trust and he dared to set aside his timidity and to step with confidence and courage into the arena.

Uta with Dandelion during his winning ride in the Grand Prix Special in Münster.

The High Point: Le Noir Wins Hearts

As Le Noir completed his training to Grand Prix, I felt a deep thankfulness to the horse and also to his owners and the many spectators that reward Le Noir and me with applause. It was never actually my declared goal to ride Grand Prix. I thought you would have to ride the horse with a lot more exertion in order to accomplish these difficult movements coming right after one another. I was surprised that my principle of riding effortlessly but effectively could be maintained with Le Noir all the way through to Grand Prix. That gave me courage to do it with the other horses. We are still astonished how far we have come!

Naturally, despite all the perfection, there is still more to be optimized with Le Noir. We polished up, for example, his Grand Prix freestyle to better bring forth Le Noir's strengths. He is really quite good at piaffe, passage, and flying changes. I would also add his feeling for rhythm that results in him becoming one with the music in the freestyle, making everything look and feel effortless. We continue to train regularly with Philip Becker, my trainer of many years. Together, we have refined the transitions from piaffe to passage as Le Noir has gained the strength to execute with suppleness this extremely demanding athletic challenge. There was still one additional challenge, namely not to overdo in riding him simply because it feels so wonderful. It is sometimes very hard to stop and not repeat an exercise for my own joy even though it was already good. A true highlight was the Grand Prix and the Grand Prix freestyle in Wiesbaden, 2012. In the previous year, we weren't invited to this show and were able to compete because Holger Schmetzer, the national coach at that time, spoke up for us. At that time, we hadn't spent much time on the international scene and the organizer didn't know us. As we won fourth in the Grand Prix and third in the freestyle, the organizer came to me in the evening and admitted that he hadn't expected such a result. I appreciated such honesty and openness, and, of course, the invitation for the next year!

Le Noir in the Grand Prix freestyle in Wiesbaden, 2012: riding a one-handed pirouette.

Uta with Le Noir

Only one year later, the audience cheered as Le Noir stepped into the flood-lit plaza in front of the castle. The commentator said, "Just a moment! Le Noir's freestyle comes next!" It was an unbelievable feeling. Everything worked. Le Noir felt great in the relaxed Wiesbaden atmosphere. Since we don't live far away, every other person knew us, and we enjoyed the fantastic mood during the whole weekend. It was just like when we stood at the fence as spectators. But this time it was our time to show, and it ran perfectly. Every movement was so good that I said to myself it couldn't be better. Le Noir managed to do the two-tempis in time with the music, and we were also able to show the one-handed canter pirouettes again. Then came our special walk routine which, as described earlier, is interrupted by the piaffe. After the piaffe, Le Noir went so relaxed into a strong walk as if we were returning to the barn after a pleasant amble through the pasture. Three meters farther, we did a second piaffe, collected him, and cantered on into the stretch of changes. Pure delight! It shot through my head that through our training we had made his over-eagerness into an advantage. The bar for effortless riding was now set very high for other horses, very high. Le Noir is simply "without words." I will never have another.

Acknowledgments

So now we have written another book, although we thought the story was already told after our success with our first title. Perhaps we dared to write the book out of pure self-interest? If yes, it was not to become rich and famous. We are a long way away from the Harry Potter books. But we are still rich in terms of experiences and acquaintances.

For example, I was asked to appear with Pat Parelli at a huge event. That was a spectacular experience. We never would have met so many interesting people in our whole lives if we hadn't written a book. And I never would have had the opportunity to help develop a special saddle. The publication was an accelerator for many other interesting encounters: with Ingrid Klimke, who we talked into doing a guest column, or Richard Hinrichs, whom we have cited in many places. We also met Harry Boldt and are proud to stand with him and many other prominent riders and experts on the authors list of the FN—the German National Equestrian Federation. The many contacts with readers have also enriched us. It is a big compliment to hear from them, for example, "After reading your book almost everything has changed for me." That is what makes one rich from writing books, even when you aren't J.K. Rowling.

But we don't want to lose sight of whom we have to thank for all this, namely our horses! And behind our horses stand their owners who believed in us and their horses. Le Noir's owner Christiane and Hans Herzog, who never sold Le Noir, despite high offers, because they were convinced that he would develop best in our hands.

And Damon Jerome's owner, Professor Hitschold, who resisted buyers from outside the country and likewise let DJ stay in our program. And Dandelion's new owner, who bought him to trail ride a little, doubting that he could achieve much.

We have had so much happiness with our owners. The owners of our other training horses were so understanding when we placed their horses into the hands of our experienced riders during the show season. The ability of the Gut Rothenkircherhof colleagues to work together as a team is a critical part of our success.

Thank you to the guest contributors that have so enriched enriched this book: Hannelore Brenner, Georg Frerich, Christoph Hess, Richard Hinrichs, Ingrid Klimke, Britta Näpel, Pat Parelli, and Dr. Angelika Trabert. We would also like to thank Angelika Frömming and Bärbel Grundmann for their valuable suggestions regarding the manuscript. They helped to make it complete.

Thank you to my husband, Stefan Schneider, for his expert support, especially in the area of starting the young horse. And thank you to our team at the Rothen-kircherhof, who had the horses clean and mud-free at the photo shoots.

A special thanks to our publishers for a wonderful collaboration!

Additionally, we would like to thank our readers. Your comments and letters, our interactions at events and shows, have broadened our horizons and opened our eyes still further. That is a valuable win that helps us to keep going, to keep on sharpening our own points of view, and to keep improving for the horses. Regardless of the level we are at, there is always a lot of room for improvement! We would like to hear from you again if you have read this book to the end. Until next time…

Uta Gräf and Friederike Heidenhof

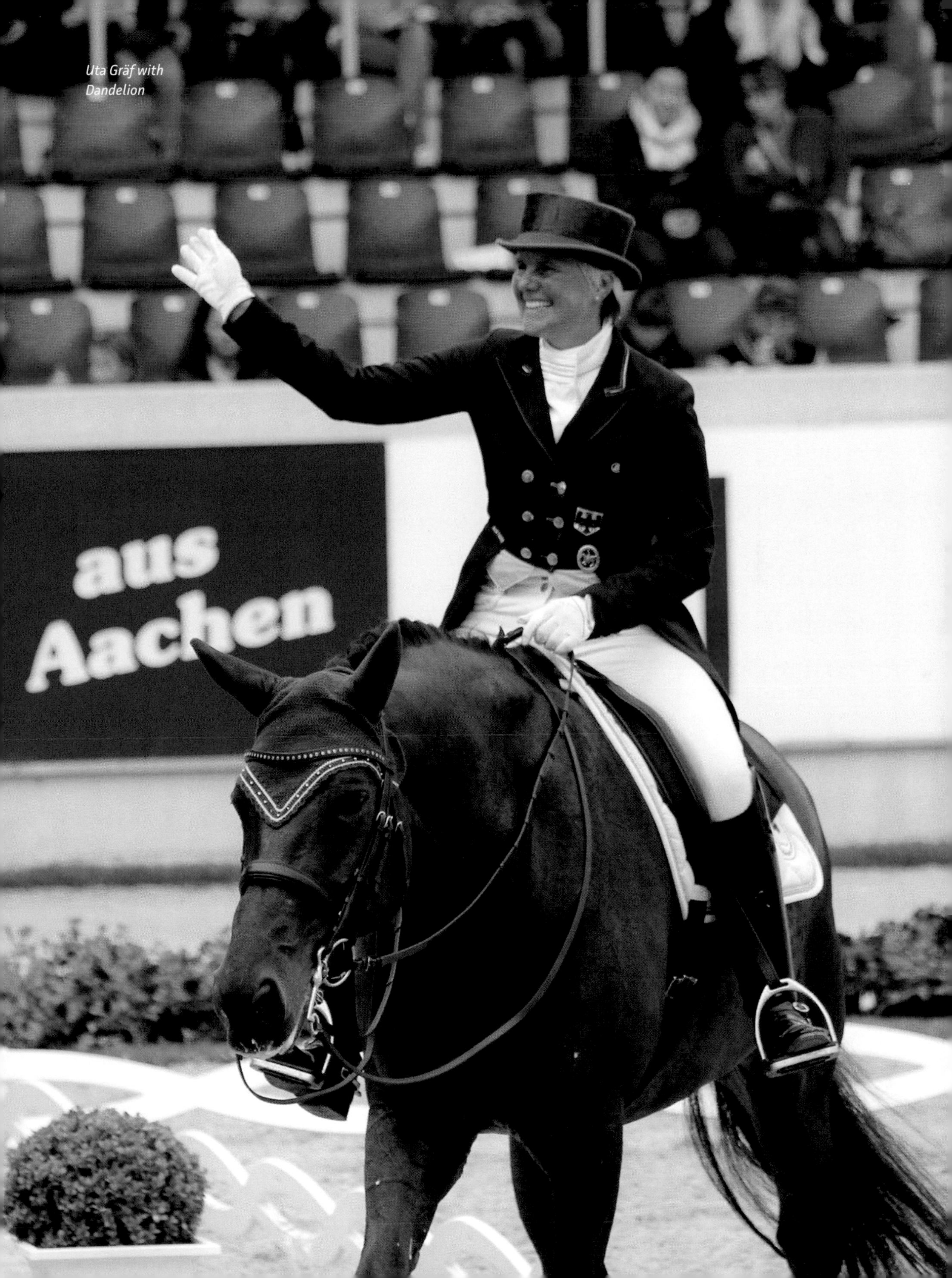

Uta Gräf with Dandelion

"Treasure Trove" with interesting tips from experts.

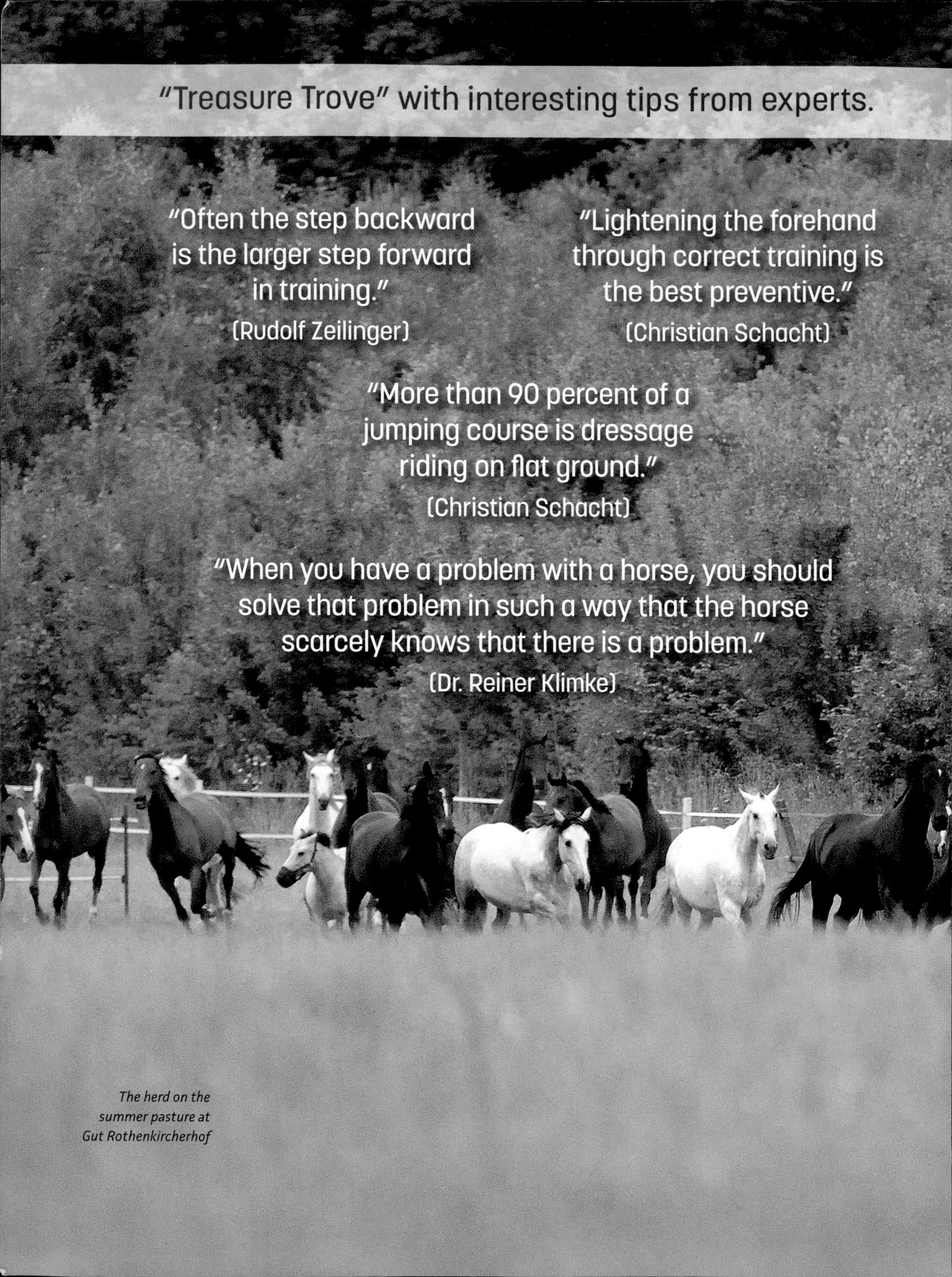

"Often the step backward is the larger step forward in training."
(Rudolf Zeilinger)

"Lightening the forehand through correct training is the best preventive."
(Christian Schacht)

"More than 90 percent of a jumping course is dressage riding on flat ground."
(Christian Schacht)

"When you have a problem with a horse, you should solve that problem in such a way that the horse scarcely knows that there is a problem."
(Dr. Reiner Klimke)

The herd on the summer pasture at Gut Rothenkircherhof

"Intelligence helps riding.
We should try to be the more
intelligent one."

(Frank R. Henning)

"When riding we should remember
variety so that the horse doesn't get
bored."

(Ingrid Klimke)

"Horses weren't born to be ridden.
They allow it. Consequently, we have
a great responsibility to our horses."

(Frank R. Henning)

Index